Victorian Entertaining

Victorian Entertaining

John Crosby Freeman

COURAGE
BOOKS

AN IMPRINT OF RUNNNG PRESS
PHILADELPHIA, PENNSYLVANIA

A RUNNNING PRESS/FRIEDMAN GROUP BOOK

Copyright © 1993, 1989 by Michael Friedman Publishing Group, Inc.

9 8 7 6 5 4 3 2 1

Digit on the right indicates the number of this printing.

VICTORIAN ENTERTAINING
was prepared and produced by
Michael Friedman Publishing Group, Inc.
15 West 26th Street
New York, New York 10010

Art Director: Robert W. Kosturko
Designer: Marcena J. Mulford
Photography Editor: Christopher C. Bain
Photography Researcher: Daniella Jo Nilva

Typeset by Mar+x Myles Graphics, Inc.
Color separations by Universal Colour Scanning Ltd.
Printed in Hong Kong by Leefung-Asco Printers Ltd.

Published by Courage Books
An imprint of Running Press
125 South Twenty-second Street
Philadelphia, Pennsylvania 19103

DEDICATION AND ACKNOWLEDGMENTS

TO THE LADIES, especially: Carolyn Flaherty, my editor at
Victorian Homes magazine, for her loyal and enthusiastic friendship;
Ruth Sunderlin Freeman, my mother, for her Yankee traditions,
dining by candlelight, and my first paying job—setting the table
for two cents; Judith Ann Schott Freeman, my wife, for her
Pennsylvania German traditions, fine linens, excellent cookery, and
the best contract I ever made—now in its twenty-fifth year;
and our daughters, Christina Crosby (5) and Rachel Lengel (3)
whose fondness for candlelight, linens, and tea parties assures us
that they will carry the old traditions of entertaining
into the twenty-first century.

CONTENTS

CONTENTS

Autumn

Summer

THE PLEASURE OF COMPANY

The aim of this book is to indicate how to entertain company at breakfast, lunch, and dinner. Too many receipts are avoided. There are generally only two or three really good modes of cooking a material, and one becomes bewildered and discouraged in trying to select and practice from books which contain from a thousand to three thousand receipts.

Mary Henderson,
Practical Cooking and Dinner Giving, 1876

ENTERTAINING IS A MEMORY BUSINESS BECAUSE the pleasures of your hospitality become immortal in the memories of your guests. The business of this book is to revive memorable Victorian entertainments to preserve the pleasure of company.

In old cities as well as rural villages overrun by suburban growth, there has been remarkable neighborhood and community revival recently. Old homes in these places look "Victorian," although many were built between 1900 and 1940. During workdays, the new generation of occupants often settle for fast food at home and away; but for entertaining family and friends on weekends and holidays, they require something special at home. Many of them get curious about their Victorian homes and obey the romantic imperative to adjust decor and lifestyle accordingly.

I know what it's like to be Old House Poor. That's why I've tried to be realistic and practical about my suggestions for Victorian entertainments. Cheap and plentiful butlers, waiters, maids, and cooks that made running the big Victorian homes possible disappeared long ago. Today, only caterers, professional entertainers, and the very wealthy can afford them. But you can still entertain in the Victorian manner, without a big budget and professional help: allow your facilities and abilities to govern the number of guests;

share responsibilities with some or all of your guests; make the service "family style" or a buffet; follow the seasonal calendar of Victorian entertainments presented in this book. Many glad surprises await you.

The mythologies of the three basic American holidays of Thanksgiving, Christmas, and the Fourth of July are Victorian and continue to be commonly celebrated with Victorian menus. Other Victorian parties are a Kentucky Derby Buffet, Burns Birth-Night Supper, Queen Victoria's Birthday High Tea, and Henley Royal Regatta Buffet. Some Victorian holidays that might be revitalized are May Day with a breakfast, Arbor Day with a garden party luncheon, and Decoration Day with a picnic. You might replace the modern madness of New Year's Eve with the neighborly delights of a Victorian New Year's Day Buffet. Or you could substitute the Victorian bonfires, fireworks, "pumpkin effigies," and autumnal feast of a Guy Fawkes Day Supper for the contemporary mischief of Halloween. At other times you might enjoy the simple pleasures of a winter breakfast, tea for two, skating and dessert, a children's tea party, a wheelmen's verandah breakfast, a lawn games luncheon, a shore dinner,

a hunt or tally-ho breakfast, a tea dance, or a casino dessert for an evening at cards. Finally, the more complex pleasures of a Victorian tent wedding breakfast or luncheon could be adapted to an anniversary or graduation supper.

An Invitation to Victorian Entertaining

This double dozen of Victorian entertainments are basic cakes for you to embellish in personal ways to create unique Victorian celebrations. For example, if you and your guests like music, you might honor Victorian composers. They don't have to be heavies; consider the popular music of Gilbert and Sullivan or Stephen Foster, and stage some patter songs or barbershop quartets. Rent a player piano and pump out "golden oldies" performed by Late Victorian and Edwardian pianists. You might honor a famous Victorian performer such as Jenny Lind, "the Swedish Nightingale."

© Brian Vanden Brink

Any theme will increase your knowledge about the period and make you a better Victorian entertainer. Almost any sector of life can have its own Victorian entertainment. It depends on what personally interests you and your guests and what is readily available to you. Consider a boat ride on an old canal, scenic lake, or river—maybe on a paddle-wheel steamer; take a ride on an old railroad train; hike along a famous trail; have a peak experience with a famous mountain in a Victorian resort area. Hold a "Captains of Capitalism" monopoly costume party. Have a "Smoke-Filled Room" cigar-sampling (for both men and women) around election time and feature Victorian Election Cake in a dessert party.

The only feature of original Victorian entertaining to be avoided today, unless agreed upon by common consent, is Victorian sexism. If you study the pictures of Victorian banquets, you rarely find ladies present. Victorian husbands occasionally invited their cronies to an all-male fish dinner at home. The presence of a wife was necessary to guarantee proper behavior by the servants and the male company, but she did not eat. According to Mrs. Henderson, it's easy to understand why. At the end of these all-fish menus, she said, "one might write *nightmare!*"

Victorian sexism cut both ways. Victorian luncheon and tea meant "Ladies' Lunch" and "Ladies' Tea." If you hold these kinds of Victorian events now, make them appealing to gentlemen as well as ladies. It's curious that most entertaining guides published in the 1980s are still written with the

Victorian assumption of an audience of hostesses. Why should today's hosts be denied the pleasures and duties of entertaining formerly reserved for ladies? Or, to put it another way, if two bring home the bacon, shouldn't two fry it up in the pan?

Victorian cookbooks often provided seasonal menus, thereby continuing a practice that began much earlier. But it was Victorian commercial canning and railroad transport that first broke down the ancient barriers of time and space governing the availability of various foods. Today, the jumbo jet has virtually eliminated all consideration of local and regional seasonality of foods. One of the practical benefits of entertaining Victorian style is a rationale for avoiding expensive, imported novelties in favor of fresh local foods. To honor the old tradition of regional foods in season, this book begins with Winter, the season characterized by home preserves and root cellar vegetables, and ends with Autumn, the season of bountiful harvest.

Victorian entertaining also allows you to avoid the expense, liabilities, and other shortcomings of that twentieth-century entertainment called "the cocktail party" or "drinks." Today, it is increasingly recognized that the cocktail party creates an imbalance of alcohol in the classic entertainment triad of food, fellowship, and spirits. Victorian entertaining is an opportunity to put them back into balance.

Mrs. Beeton borrowed the admirable system of setting out the ingredients, the quantities, and the timing of the recipes in the uniform and concise manner [from Eliza Acton whose] Modern Cookery, published by Longmans in 1845, was the first English cookery book in which such instructions were given. Her methodical mind and meticulous honesty made her cookery book then, and makes it even still, far and away the most admired in the English language.

Elizabeth David,
An Omelette and a Glass of Wine, 1985

The most important measuring device in a Victorian kitchen was a balance beam scale; it was the substitute for today's measuring cups and spoons. Sometimes I have emphasized the proportional relationships of a recipe. These relationships, along with accumulated cookery wisdom, made it possible for Victorian cooks to carry so much in their heads. As Elizabeth David points out, weights of ingredients and their inter-relationships are the keys to great baking because it enables bakers to cope with variations in eggs, shortenings, and flours. This is the method Mrs. Beeton used in her cake recipe for Victoria Sandwiches, which you find in the Little Girl's Tea Party.

With the exception of the "Winter Breakfast," there is no extensive food history in this book. Instead, I have focused on "feature food," suggesting a festive food typically associated with a particular entertainment or its season, to which you can add your own supplemental dishes. Not all popular Victorian entertainment foods were mentioned because some of them, like canvasback duck and terrapin, are no longer commonly available. Nor did I feature all the typically Victorian entertainments because some of them, like galas and balls, would put you at the mercy of expensive caterers and entertainment advisors; others, like "calls" and "at homes," are obsolete. My purpose has been to suggest foods and entertainments that provide an accessible and useable Victorian past for the pleasure of company.

Ideas from Practical Cooking and Dinner Giving

Mary Henderson, whose no-nonsense entertaining advice is drawn upon throughout this book, was a St. Louis hostess professionally trained in Paris, London, and New York cooking schools. Over a century after it was written, the common sense of her 1876 book, *Practical Cooking and Dinner Giving*, still merits consideration. As a reviewer in the *New York Evening Post* said, she "gives many useful instructions concerning the art of entertaining, some of which will help housekeepers to avoid what [famous nineteenth-century essayist] Charles Lamb called 'roast lady' with their dinners."

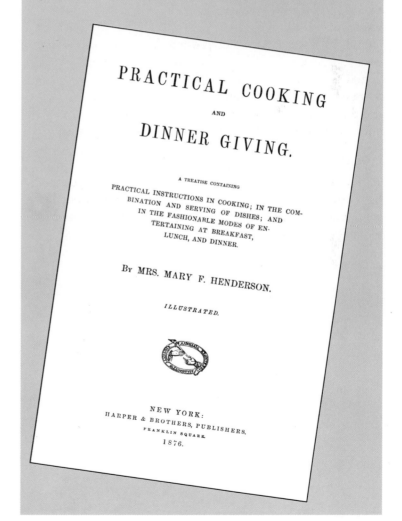

PRACTICAL COOKING
AND
DINNER GIVING.

A TREATISE CONTAINING
PRACTICAL INSTRUCTIONS IN COOKING; IN THE COMBINATION AND SERVING OF DISHES; AND IN THE FASHIONABLE MODES OF ENTERTAINING AT BREAKFAST, LUNCH, AND DINNER.

BY MRS. MARY F. HENDERSON.

ILLUSTRATED.

NEW YORK:
HARPER & BROTHERS, PUBLISHERS,
FRANKLIN SQUARE.
1876.

Winter

VICTORIAN CHRISTMAS

*My thoughts are drawn back, by a fascination which I
do not care to resist, to my own childhood. I begin to
consider, what do we all remember best upon the branches of the
Christmas Tree of our own young Christmas days, by which we
climbed to real life.*

Charles Dickens,
A Christmas Tree

MEMORIES ARE FOREVER, AND FEW ARE MORE powerful than those of childhood. Christmas is the quintessential children's festival, for which we can thank three Victorians. One was English. Two were American.

VICTORIAN CHRISTMAS MYTHOLOGIES

G.K. Chesterton said Dickens "was the last of the mythologists, and perhaps the greatest." But there's more to Victorian children's Christmas than Dickens's 1843 *Christmas Carol* morality play about capitalist wealth, shown every year on TV to compromise the religious and secular celebrations of Christmas. More childlike is his *Christmas Tree*, a richly detailed inventory of gifts and fantasies.

Santa Claus comes from the old Dutch "Sinterklaas," but his mythology is *The Night Before Christmas*, written in 1822 by Clement Moore, a professor of Hebrew at New York's General Theological Seminary, for his children. Thomas Nast was better known in his own time as a political cartoonist for *Harper's Weekly*, but his Christmas illustrations of a fat and jovial Santa Claus based on Moore's poetry have lasted far longer than his cartoons.

Victorian Christmas ornaments are a fashionable collectible; many have been reproduced.

Today's shrinking living spaces, as well as rising purchase and disposal costs for trees, have made the Victorian table-top Christmas tree necessary as well as fashionable. Like bigger floor-to-ceiling trees, table-top trees were decorated by adults and then revealed to the children.

Gathered around the Wassail Bowl, everyone will be caught by the holiday spirit.

One way that British Victorians coped with modern realities was to mythologize their rural, medieval history. That's why Victorian adult Christmas combined the Victorian religion of Domesticity with the Romantic revival of Merrie Olde England. As a mythologist of Christmas, Washington Irving—America's first author to achieve fame in England—beat the British Romantics to the punch in 1819. His *Sketches by Geoffrey Crayon* of an old English Christmas were published fifteen years before Dickens' *Pickwick*.

Yule Logs, Wassail Bowls, and Parading the Boar's Head were, for most Victorians, memories perpetuated by Olde English carols. Victorian central heating made big and smoky medieval fireplaces burning Yule logs obsolete; Victorians used them as symbolic ancestral hearths fired up with lesser timber on ceremonial occasions like Christmas. Wassail, a richly spiced and highly sweetened punch made with robust ale, wine, or cider, had too much clout for Victorian palates accustomed to more subtle beverages. "The boar's head in hand bear I" has been sung every Christmas at Queen's College, Oxford, but most Victorians substituted a parade of the roast turkey or goose.

© Dane T. Wells

Expensive antique or reproduction ornaments aren't necessary for a delightful Victorian Christmas tree. This one was decorated with homemade baked goods, paper flowers, and baskets of candy by Connie Hershey for the Queen Victoria Inn in Cape May, New Jersey. Note the portrait of Her Majesty and the Bradbury reproduction wallpaper of Pugin's crown-and-thistle pattern for Balmoral Castle.

CHRISTMAS MENUS

Parading the Turkey is one of many Victorian Christmas traditions that survive in the twentieth century. Today's Christmas menu still features home preserves and root cellar vegetables like potatoes, squash, and carrots. To innovate, you might do an old Christmas vegetable in a new way using Marian Morash's excellent 1982 *Victory Garden Cookbook*. Or you might explore other Victorian Christmas meats, desserts, and beverages.

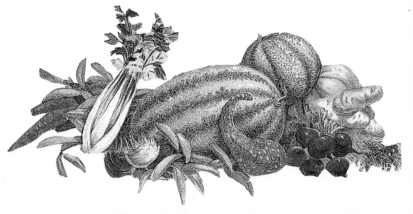

Parading the Turkey is the modern equivalent of the medieval Parading the Boar's Head. Franklin failed to make turkey the national symbol of the U.S., but Americans honor their bird, which is wily and hard to bag in the wild, during festive occasions like Christmas.

Crown Roast of Pork

To trump the turkey and reserve it for Thanksgiving when it has greater symbolic significance, consider that grand Victorian convenience—Crown Roast of Pork. It costs more, requiring a pair of loins and an experienced butcher to create an attractive crown, but it has more impact. Make sausage from the trimmings and put it in the crown to flavor and moisten the roast; perhaps your butcher might mix it to your specifications. If your family suffers from carving anxiety, this is the cure because your butcher has done most of the work. Likewise banished is the muddle of who gets what. It's a simple matter to sever and serve the individual chops.

The Soup Course

Victorians often served sherry with consommé and other light soups. Turn this to practical advantage while your guests are waiting for the last one to arrive. In place of twentieth-century cocktails and nibbles, serve guests the Victorian soup course in old bouillon cups or fancy teacups along with little glasses of sherry. In the absence of hired help, this also avoids the clumsiness of removing the soup course.

Stilton is the king of cheeses and a powerful finish to any festive meal.

Stilton

"Dessert without cheese is the kiss without the squeeze" is a suggestive piece of Victorian advice. The squeeze for Christmas is Stilton, a copyrighted cheese needled into perfection and limited by law to the English counties of Leicester, Derby, and Nottingham. Don't ruin Stilton with port poured into holes; put the port into yourself. Carefully slice off

the top of the Stilton wheel and reserve it. Cut a layer about an inch or so thick, wedge it into individual servings, and pass it on an elegant glass plate. When served at table, neatly surround the unappetizing surface of this great cheese with a white napkin.

Water versus Wine

Since most Victorian pump or tap water was unreliable, good wine was often a substitute for bad water. Fashionable homes had a large, decorative, metal water cooler with a charcoal filter. Iced water was an option available from a special pitcher on the sideboard. Victorian entertaining provides the opportunity to bring wine and food back into balance as well as revive the Victorian tradition of serving madeira or port.

Madeira and Port

It's impossible to reproduce historic meals; today's tastes wouldn't approve even if we could. But you *can* capture history in a bottle. Christmas pudding and other Victorian desserts were often served with a small glass of madeira or port. Excellent examples of these rich and sweet wines are still available. If money is no object, you could buy a nineteenth-century madeira or port and almost be guaranteed it's as good as ever. For much less you can get younger bottles of these Portuguese wines that will take you back just as well. They must be decanted to separate the sediment. Because the wine could be stored from one meal to the next, Victorian decanters remained visible on the table or sideboard. Sometimes they had cut glass facets that glittered in the light and enhanced the colors of the wine.

Port and madeira were served in small glasses and sipped slowly. Today, most people will be ill-prepared to receive it if they have been drinking other wines throughout the meal. Madeira and port will also be compromised by the candylike sweetness of today's desserts. Your plum pudding, for example, should have no added sugar and its sauce should not be too sweet.

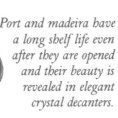

Cake Versus Bread

Homemade yeast breads repay the effort recently reduced by food processors and mixers with dough hooks. Many bread-makers say the final hand-kneeding is great therapy—a kind of Zen serenity comes with the rhythm. The bible is Elizabeth David's *English Bread and Yeast Cookery*, available in a 1980 American edition edited by Karen Hess. Derivation of "the upper crust" is revealed in her chapter on "manchet"—the ancestral soft, white loaf that has dwindled into today's damp Kleenex of commerce. Servants' guides of the sixteenth century specify that manchet must always be cut so the softer or upper crust is given to the Lord. Perhaps this is also "the cut above"?

Port and madeira have a long shelf life even after they are opened and their beauty is revealed in elegant crystal decanters.

Today, the noble association of soft white bread is being replaced by darker, heartier, more healthy, wholegrain breads. This emphasis on the importance on good bread has renewed the ancient symbolism of bread as good fellowship. Take a moment at the beginning of your Victorian Christmas and other gatherings of your family and friends to celebrate the simple pleasure of being together by "breaking bread." If yeast bread is beyond you, blueberry, date, or corn muffins can be made easily.

© Dick Dietrich/FPG International

So long as she has puff pastry, rich black cake, clear jelly and preserves, she considers that such unimportant matters as bread, butter, and meat may take care of themselves. [This] inattention to common things leads people to build houses with stone fronts, and window-caps and expensive front-door trimmings, without bathing-rooms or fireplaces, or ventilators.

Beecher and Stowe,
American Woman's Home, 1869

This 1876 Harper's Weekly *wood-engraving shows Christmas Pudding presided over by a mother who makes a rare appearance in the kitchen to teach her children the old family recipe.*

Plum Pudding

Victorians believed Christmas Plum Pudding was "the triumph of the housewife's art"—the one dish every mother should teach every daughter to make. Boiled pudding, like soup and stew, is one of the world's oldest preparations. The tart plums originally used in medieval European Christmas puddings were eventually replaced by sweeter dried grapes from Greece like the "Zante currant," which is still available. "In cakes and puddings this delicious little grape is most extensively used; in fact, we could not make a *plum* pudding without the currant," according to *Beeton's Household Management,* 1861.

Some plum pudding recipes call for sultanas—originally Turkish raisins made from golden yellow, seedless grapes. Mixed candied peel completes the fruits. Suet, a leaf lard found around the kidneys and loins of beef, is the traditional shortening. (Your butcher should have suet or ask the meat department at your grocery store to get what you need.) Quantities of eggs leaven the pudding. These ingredients provide ample opportunity for adjusting proportions to create "an old family recipe."

Mrs. Beeton's Christmas Plum Pudding

Ingredients:—1 $^{1}/_{2}$ lb. of raisins, $^{1}/_{2}$ lb. of currants, $^{1}/_{2}$ lb. of mixed peel, $^{3}/_{4}$ lb. bread crumbs, $^{3}/_{4}$ lb. suet, 8 eggs, 1 wineglassful of brandy.

Use some brandy to plump the fruit. Lightly flour the suet while mincing it and lightly dredge the currants and raisins; it keeps the suet and fruit from sticking to itself, and the fruit from sinking to the bottom. Eggs are beaten into a froth. Fold the combined dry ingredients into the eggs and brandy. Put mixture in a clean, lightly floured cloth bag, knotting the top around a long wooden or plastic spoon. Suspend it in a kettle of boiling water five or six hours. A mold may yield a somewhat prettier pudding, but a bag gives better results. If you use a mold or don't suspend the bag, put an inverted plate in the bottom to keep the pudding from burning and sticking. You can make your own pudding bags from sheets or pillowcases.

Pudding was one of the original convenience foods—the first boil-in-a-bag dessert. Many were made at one time because they stored well in old cellars that were cool and moist. (Today, wrap and refrigerate to prevent drying.) Ease of reheating was their chief attraction. Surprise winter parties had instant dessert by yanking a bagged pudding off a cellar peg and plunging it into boiling water for an hour or two to reheat. Today's leftovers, sliced into individual servings, can be microwaved.

TABLE GRACE

Victorian families usually said a table grace; Christmas dinner is a rare occasion when modern families feel compelled to follow suit. Don't wait for all to be served. No sensate mind can rise to Heaven above while delightful aromas are dragging it down to Paradise on the plate. Victorians had more common sense; they served the words before they served the food. After the hostess received, if she was not helping the service, or after the guest of honor received, she told the next person served to begin.

Few were as successful as Cecil Aldin in illustrating Irving's and Dickens's Victorian romanticism of Merrie Olde England (top). This charming picture of amiable fellowship is a reminder that the toast is a convivial form of table grace. Bring out the best for your family—linens, china, crystal—and holiday spirit will shine throughout your home (above).

© Brian Vanden Brink

NEW YEAR'S DAY BUFFET

On that genial day the fountains of hospitality were broken up, and the whole community was deluged with cherry brandy, true Hollands, and mulled cider; every house was a temple to the jolly god; and many a provident vagabond got drunk out of pure economy, taking in liquor enough gratis to serve him half a year afterwards.

Washington Irving,
Diedrich Knickerbocker's History of New York, 1809

IRVING WAS EXAGGERATING, BUT ENOUGH kirsch, gin, and spiced apple wine flowed in New Amsterdam during this old Dutch holiday to make it true. Edith Wharton's *New Year's Day* (1924) recalls how fashionable New York families like hers "no longer received" in the 1870s. Instead of being absent from town to avoid the parvenus who continued the custom, "Grandmamma marked the day by a family reunion, a kind of supplementary Christmas." Today, this is how most Americans celebrate New Year's Day.

Samuel Hopkins Adams remembers "A Third Ward New Year's" in his *Grandfather Stories* (1955). The year is 1881, the place is a fashionable neighborhood in Rochester, New York; he is ten, and it is his social "debut." New Year's Day was Neighborhood Open House. Each home had a specialty: one had a dessert table for the children with a massive Charlotte Russe centerpiece; another was known "for that meatiest of rare luxuries, scalloped oysters." Doors of homes deliberately vacated for the day held baskets to receive calling cards. In the street talk of the day, these houses were "N.G." (No Grub).

"New Year's Day in New York" from an 1859 Harper's Weekly *(above) shows how females remained at home and males made visits or "calls." The reception and buffet is in a double parlor, fashionably decorated with large paintings in gilded frames, ornate window dressings, wall-to-wall carpet, and two gas chandeliers. The large urn on the buffet might be dispensing a bracing broth or a sobering beverage, but the fellow nearby with his glass raised high suggests that most gentlemen preferred the alcohol. The young couple behind him show that New Year's Day was also an opportunity for some genteel horseplay.*

Hand coloring by Melissa Dehncke

NEW YEAR'S NEIGHBORHOOD VISITING DAY

This is a Victorian entertainment whose time has returned. Victorian Lovers are doing more today than fixing up old houses for their new families; they are repairing neighborhoods and communities. New Year's Day Visiting is the occasion for rebuilding and celebrating the good fellowship where you live. Start with a street, parish, historic district, or local amenity society. Share the burden and the fun by changing the roster each year. Make it a fund-raiser for a nonprofit organization and get free publicity, volunteer help, donation of quality foodstuffs for showcasing, and funding for the costs of food and labor.

One of the reasons Victorian homes are so wonderful is the richness of their design details and color schemes. As you visit your Victorian-loving friends on New Year's Day, take time to stop and look closely at each part of their homes.

Calling Cards

Blank calling cards would make meaningful tour tickets. Provide one for each house on the tour that is "receiving," write the name of the "caller" on each card, and collect them at the door. It's worth the effort. If they are perceived as calling cards instead of tour tickets, people will tend to obey their obligations as individual guests instead of demand their rights as a tourist group.

A Boston gentleman got into his carriage to make some calls and discovered he had forgotten his calling cards. He told his new and inexperienced footman to go to the parlor mantel-piece and get the cards that were there. The servant found there a pack of playing-cards and thought those were the ones.
The number of "not at home" places where the footman was sent in with a card made the gentleman anxious. "How many cards have you left?" he asked. "Well," said the footman, "the ace of hearts is all that remains." "The deuce!" exclaimed the master. "I left the deuce in the last house," was the reply.

Harper's Weekly, December 30, 1876

Victorian preprinted cards with blank spaces for the penning of names were popular. Although it was a century that admired "a fine hand," there was small social gain, if any, from engraved cards. Today, calligraphy has been revived as a popular art form, so there are many study guides and practice materials available. Victorian entertainers might lead by example and stimulate their regular guests to make personal calling cards in a Victorian style. They would be pretty mementoes of special occasions that could be handed down to future generations in a handsome memory book. Try the one published by Running Press in 1987, called *Occasions Remembered: An Entertainment Diary.*

Calling cards varied widely in expense and graphics, from handwritten, to rubber-stamped, or pre-printed cards, to deeply embossed, brightly colored, and richly gilded cards sometimes mounted with hinged overlays. They survive in today's business cards, as well as in military leaders who are still described in a Victorian fashion as "officers and gentlemen."

© Dennis Gottlieb

FAMILY DINNER FOR NEW YEAR'S DAY

As Edith Wharton suggested, a Victorian family New Year's Day was "little Christmas" minus the gifts. According to William Woys Weaver's 1983 *Sauerkraut Yankees*, even the Quakers approved of this celebration. In Pennsylvania, he says, goose was for Christmas and turkey with sauerkraut was for New Year's Day. It was also customary on that day to eat sauerkraut with pork "because, as the Dutch say, 'the pig roots *forward*.'"

Pork, like many main course meats, is more for eating than looking; therefore the table setting must work its magic. If your tabletop is superb, you are naturally reluctant to cover it with a cloth; elegant mats, which Victorians often placed on top of cloths, satisfy the requirement. If your porcelain is richly colored and ornamented, use mats with a neutral field. Any table is enhanced by candlelight.

A NEW YEAR'S DAY BUFFET

Escaloped oysters, cold tongue, turkey, chicken, and ham, pressed meats, boned turkey, jellied chicken; sandwiches or wedding sandwich rolls; pickled oysters, chicken and lobster salads, cold slaw garnished with fried oysters; bottled pickles, French or Spanish pickles; jellies; charlotte russe, ice-creams, ices; two large handsome cakes for decoration of table, and one or two baskets of mixed cake, fruit, layer, and sponge cake predominating; fruits; nuts; coffee, chocolate with whipped cream, lemonade.

Practical Housekeeping, Minneapolis, 1881

For New Year's Day, fill your table with luscious dishes served on your best china. What could be better than beginning the year with good cheer and fellowship?

© Carson T. Zullinger/Rockwood Museum

VICTORIAN SKATING PARTY

A huge bonfire near the riverbank was kept at a high blaze by brush from an adjoining wood lot. It lighted up the figures of men and women, gliding, darting, and swooping upon the glass-smooth ice. Bedded in embers from the fire, a large iron kettle simmered and steamed with water to be used to prepare the hot, buttered rum which was the inspiration and support of such occasions.

Samuel Hopkins Adams,
"The Saga of Four-Skate Pilkington,"
in *Grandfather Stories*, 1955

The fancy dress and architecture in this illustration implies skating was a winter sport for Victorian gentry, but skates that could be strapped on to one's shoes were not expensive. Skating was an ancient European sport brought to America with the Dutch settlement of New York. Skating in New York's Central Park made the sport fashionable before the Civil War.

ICE SKATING—IT'S AN ANCIENT EXCUSE TO escape the sour and dusty prisons of heated interiors and leap into the clean winter air. It's also a Victorian sweet excuse for making old-fashioned treats. Think of this event as an outdoor Winter dessert party with nut fudge, mulled cider, hot chocolate, and popcorn balled with hot taffy. Are these childish things? Absolutely! For many, they were the first experience with the magic of cooking.

CREATE A SKATING RINK

Even in a densely populated city, with some planning you can could create a skating rink for a day. Ask local firemen to flood an empty lot or a corner of a parking area vacant on a Sunday afternoon or part of a public park or the end of a street closed off for a block party. You will need a portable shelter and stove for making the treats. In a suburban yard, it shouldn't be too much effort to make a rink with some stakes, boards, and sturdy plastic sheeting.

The Victorian equivalent of dressing for the slopes was dressing for the rinks. Victorian skating was popular amongst the young for the same reason skiing is today—fresh opportunities for new friendships outside the conventional boundaries of society.

Hot Buttered Rum

An adult beverage often found at Victorian skating parties is that old Colonial favorite, Hot Buttered Rum. Using a ceramic mug will avoid the risk of breaking a glass with boiling water. In the bottom of each mug dissolve a lump of sugar with a little boiling water. Add a jigger of dark rum, then fill the mug with boiling water. Float a pat of butter, unsalted if possible, on top. You can spice this drink with some nutmeg or provide each mug with a cinnamon swizzle stick. Candy is dandy but on a bitter winter day, hot buttered rum is salvation itself!

Mulled Cider

The operative spices in mulled cider are cinnamon, cloves, and allspice. If you start with the homemade apple wine some call "hard" cider, you may want to sweeten a half gallon (2 liters) of it with up to one half cup (100 grams) delicately-flavored honey. If you want to "harden" a half gallon (2 liters) of sweet cider, you can add eight to sixteen ounces (240 to 480 milliliters) of light rum, apple jack, or brandy before serving. An interesting addition would be one tablespoon (15 milliliters) or more of maple syrup. A half gallon (2 liters) of unfiltered "natural" apple juice sold in grocery stores can be substituted for unprocessed cider. Heat, but do not boil, the cider and the syrup or honey with two to four sticks of cinnamon and a cheese-cloth bag containing one half teaspoon to one teaspoon (2 to 5 milliliters) allspice and two to six whole cloves. Before serving in mugs or cups, discard the bag of spices. Some recipes also add a dash of angostura or orange bitters. Use cinnamon as swizzle sticks.

Mulled cider is an accessible and economical festive winter beverage, good with or without an alcoholic boost. The clear glass pitcher showcases its rich color.

© Steven Mark Needham/Envision

Hot Chocolate

South America's gift to the world, chocolate, like tea, coffee, sugar, and spices, has a rich history of colonialism. Until it dawned on Dutch pirates that cacao beans on seventeenth-century Spanish ships were valuable, chocolate made little headway elsewhere in Europe. Hot chocolate eventually became an expensive, fashionable drink restricted to the upper

Directions for Using
PAYN & McNAUGHTON'S
PREPARED
COCOA.

Boil a half tea-cup full in three quarts milk and water (more milk the better,) for fifteen minutes, let it settle, and it is fit for use.

classes until Victorian technology in Holland, England, Switzerland, and America made it the popular food it is today. Conrad van Houten discovered how to make cocoa powder in 1828; Fry & Sons (now Cadbury) first made chocolate candy in 1847; Nestlé made milk chocolate in 1875; and Hershey thoroughly mechanized the process at the end of the century.

Although some of the finest surviving pieces of eighteenth-century silver and porcelain are chocolate pots, most Victorian hot chocolate was poured from cheap imported china "chocolate jugs." An expensive Royal Worcester jug cost $8.50 in the 1890s, but more popular were cheaper jugs "in the Doulton style of decoration" sold at the same time for $2.75. Chocolate pots or jugs usually have straight sides that slope inwards and look like elongated and lidded tankards. For your winter skating party, serve chocolate in the cups of a chocolate set or in sturdy mugs. If you don't have a chocolate set, a tea service works just as well.

© Michael Kingsford/Envision

Today's ready-made mixes and syrups have trivialized hot chocolate into a common drink for kids. Making it from scratch is worth the effort, especially when topped with real whipped cream and chocolate shavings.

Taffy

Taffy, like most forms of candy, is boiled sugar. The basic recipe is two cups (450 grams) molasses, two teaspoons (10 milliliters) vinegar, and one half teaspoon (2.5 milliliters) baking soda. Some recipes specify the vinegar flavoring and soda be added last; others boil it with the molasses. You might add some essence of peppermint at the end instead of the vinegar. White or brown sugar was sometimes specified, but molasses was the most convenient ingredient. The mixture was boiled to "hard ball" (250 to 268 degrees F; 120 to 130 degrees C) or "soft crack" (270 degrees F; 132 degrees C), determined by dropping a spoonful in cold water or on a marble slab, where it will either form a hard ball or crack.

Shaker Molasses Taffy (*Shaker Cookbook*, 1953) combines one cup (225 grams) sugar with one cup (225 grams) molasses and is softened by adding one cup (225 grams) cream. At the end, it adds one teaspoon (5 milliliters) baking soda, two tablespoons butter (30 milliliters), and one cup (225 grams) chopped black walnuts are added. A better technique is to put the butter on your hands and work it into the taffy while pulling. Putting the nuts in at the end before final shaping will avoid grating your hands while pulling.

A uniquely North American taffy is maple sugar taffy. In this case follow the Shaker recipe and substitute one cup (225 grams) maple sugar for the molasses.

Nut Fudge

There isn't much difference between the recipes for taffy and fudge. The recipe for Shaker Molasses Taffy, with its two cups (450 grams) of sugars and one cup (225 grams) of cream minus the soda is a basic recipe for fudge. Made as fudge, this mixture is not heated as high—only "soft ball" (236 to 240 degrees F; (113 to 115 degrees C).

Avoid scraping sugar crystals on the sides of the pot into the boiling fudge. Covering the pot for a couple minutes will trap enough steam to liquify them. At "soft ball," remove the pot from the fire, add 2 tablespoons (30 milliliters) of butter, and stir the mixture vigorously with a spoon until it starts to solidify. Then stir in the chopped nuts and some vanilla and pour into a pan or molds. Score the pan of fudge into squares and press whole nuts into the centers.

How to Pull Candy

After boiling candy, turn it on a marble slab or a large meat-plate to cool. When cool, but not cold, grease your hands lightly with olive oil or butter, take the candy in your hands, throw it over a large hook and pull it towards you, and so continue until the candy is creamy. Make the candy move, and not your hands, or you will blister them quickly.

Mrs. S.T. Rorer,
Philadelphia Cook Book, 1886

Pulling taffy works air into the candy, lightening it in color and substance. It's more fun to have a pulling partner than use a hook. Each person clutches an end of the taffy, pulls it out about eighteen inches, folds it over on itself, and repeats, twisting the taffy now and then. Finally, on a surface coated with cornstarch or confectioners' sugar, pull the taffy into a long rope and cut with scissors into small pieces.

There are many store-bought candies of widely varying quality and expense today, but none can equal those you make with your children or friends at home using the best possible ingredients. No matter what Ogden Nash said about the slow results of candy, he had to admit it was "dandy."

BURNS BIRTH NIGHT

The Burns birth-night celebration was the most universal literary festival ever known. The heart of the world beat responsive to the memory of the man as it has always thrilled to his song. Homer is a myth, Dante a cloud, Shakespeare a power, but Burns is a brother man.

The New York celebration of
The Burns Centennial, *Harper's Weekly*, January 25, 1859

If poetry in general and that of Burns in particular is not your cup of tea, a comfortable chair in front of a crackling fire and frequent samplings of Burns's favorite beverage will probably change your mind.

TRADITIONAL SCOTTISH FARE

MIDWINTER NEEDS CHEERING UP, AND there's no better Victorian precedent than spending the evening of January 25 celebrating the birth of Robert Burns and all things Scottish. During the feast of Hogmanay or Scottish New Year's Eve, the haggis, an ancient Scottish boiled meat loaf pudding, is ceremonially paraded into the room like a medieval Christmas boar's head. Kilted bagpipers lead the haggis followed by a person bearing over his head a crossed pair of whisky bottles. It is traditional to toast the haggis with some lines from Burns and pour a libation of the first "wee dram" of whisky over each serving. This ceremony can be repeated on Burns Birth-Night, although it seems like a misplaced use of good whisky.

It's difficult to make the obligatory haggis, because many of the classic ingredients such as sheep offal are now routinely processed into pet food. You can approximate haggis with a hash or meat loaf.

Cock-a-leekie: A Souper Supper

An easier and equally appropriate main dish would be "Cock-a-leekie," more of a chicken stew than a leek soup. Like most stews, it used an animal that was cheap because it was no longer productive for anything else, i.e., an old cock. Today you will pay more for a tough, old bird, called a "stewing chicken," than a tender, young fryer or roaster. But its flavor is essential to cock-a-leekie. Mrs. Beeton noted, "Cock-a-leekie was largely consumed at the Burns Centenary Festival at the Crystal Palace, Sydenham, in 1859."

Leek Soup, Commonly Called Cock-A-Leekie

Ingredients—a capon or large fowl (sometimes an old cock) which should be trussed as for boiling; 2 or 3 bunches of fine leeks, 5 quarts of beef or veal stock, pepper and salt to taste.

Mode—*well wash the leeks (and, if old, scald them in boiling water for a few minutes), taking off the roots and part of the heads, and cut them into lengths of about an inch. Put the fowl into the stock, with, at first, one half of the leeks, and allow it to simmer gently. In half an hour add the remaining leeks, and then it may simmer for three or four hours longer. It should be carefully skimmed, and can be seasoned to taste. In serving, take*

out the fowl, and carve it neatly, placing the pieces in a tureen, and pouring over them the soup, which should be very thick of leeks.

Sufficient for 10 persons.

Isabella Beeton,
Book of Household Management, 1861

Note that soup should never be boiled. Theodora Fitzgibbon's *Taste of Scotland* (1970) gives a recipe that also includes chopped bacon and fines herbes cooked with the stew. It specifies twelve chopped leeks and reserves two of them for the last fifteen minutes of cooking, at which point one cup of cooked and stoned prunes are added.

Mutton ham was more common in pre-industrial days when sheep were mainly raised for wool and eaten when they were old. Smoking is an ancient preservative technique used on a variety of meats other than pork.

Mutton Ham

Mutton is harder to get these days than stewing chicken. You have to persuade a sheep farmer to keep one alive long enough to become mutton. It's not the delicate flavor of lamb you are after, it's the more robust taste of mutton. If you manage to get legs of mutton and live near a pork-processing area, ask your butcher to cure and smoke one for you like a regular ham.

Scottish vegetables that go with mutton ham are kale, rutabagas, turnips, and potatoes. Consider combining equal amounts of separately boiled potatoes and turnips mashed together with some butter and chopped chives or shallots. This makes a traditional slap-up dish from the Scottish island of Orkney delightfully named Clapshot (*Taste of Scotland*, 1971). Any of your usual companions of ham would also go well with mutton ham.

Dundee Cake

For dessert you could make a Dundee Cake, a baked version of Christmas plum pudding with glacé cherries topped with blanched split almonds and glazed with some sugared milk. Any good fruitcake recipe using quality ingredients with the cherries, almonds, and glazing would satisfy the requirement. Don't make it too sweet, and serve it with some small glasses of Drambuie—promoted by its manufacturer as "Bonnie Prince Charlie's liqueur."

Straight Malt Whisky

You can quote as much as you like Cowper's temperance piety about tea being the drink "that cheers but does not inebriate," but Burns Birth-Night is the occasion to celebrate *whisky*— the Celtic "water of life" that both cheers *and* inebriates. Wasn't one of the bonnie bard's most happy poems in praise of "Scotch Drink"? Blending expensive Highland malt whiskies with cheaper Lowland grain whiskies to make a cheaper and lighter beverage was a marketing practice begun by big Victorian distilleries. To a purist, embracing Scotch whisky by drinking blends is like being kissed by a committee.

There are dozens of straight Scotch malt whiskies, each with its own individual character. For a Burns chowder and marching society of twenty to thirty people, the expense and effort to gather a special collection of straight malt whiskies would be justified by the shared pleasure. Special wine tastings are arranged—why not a whisky tasting?

Theodora Fitzgibbon's Taste of Scotland *says "Dundee cake makes an excellent christening, wedding or Christmas cake."*

SCOTTISH ENTERTAINMENTS

The tartanizing of Scottish folklore was the Scottish equivalent of the English Victorian Gothic Revival. It began with the enormously popular Victorian novels of Sir Walter Scott that seized the romantic imagination of the world. Its biggest fans were Queen Victoria and Prince Albert, who acquired their Highland castle, Balmoral, in 1848 and redecorated it in the tartan style. Because the Act of Union between Scotland and England was still a recent memory, their Highland visits were good politics; but they also genuinely loved Balmoral, especially its privacy relative to Windsor Castle or Buckingham Palace.

If you can't schedule some kilted bagpipers for your Burns Birth-Night, don't despair. It is said that after a dram or two of good straight malt whisky, you'll see the tartans and hear the skirl of the bagpipes.

© E. Nagele/FPG International

Dessert and Cards

If dinner is too expensive or time-consuming and the flow of whisky threatens to make the celebration too rowdy, which it probably was during much of the nineteenth century, substitute a bridge party. Model it after the 1920s "Scotch Card Party" found in *The Calendar of Entertainments* by Wallis and Gates: "Invitations might parody a well-known verse from the Scotch poet: 'Gin a body ask a body/On Bobbie Burns' day/For a friendly game of cards/Need a body's friend say nay?'" Purchase plaid note paper or correspondence cards. Match partners by cutting swatches of different plaids in half and having guests take a piece from a plaid gingham bag. Name tables or teams for famous clans. Keep score with pins inserted into thistles made from a foam ball covered with lavender cloth.

Queen Victoria and Prince Albert genuinely loved the Highlands, and they popularized Scottish culture.

The prize could be a secondhand copy of Burns freshened by a new book jacket made from plaid cloth.

Petticoat Tails

Since this would be a dessert party, you might feature "Petticoat Tails," allegedly a favorite of Mary, Queen of Scots. The classic recipe calls for about five times more flour than butter, sweetened with some sugar, moistened with some milk, and spiced with some caraway seeds. Your favorite sugar cookie recipe could be substituted. Cut the rolled-out dough into circles using an inverted dinner plate as a form; cut a circle out of the center with a small inverted glass and leave the dough in place; score the dough outside the inner circle with a knife into eight or more segments that, after baking, are broken apart into the "petticoat tail" shapes.

WINTER BREAKFAST

Courtesy Motif Designs

A cozy breakfast setting for two refreshes the concept of romantic dining. The food can be as simple or splendid as you please.

Dinner parties are mere formalities; but you may invite a man to breakfast because you want to see him.

Thomas Babbington Macaulay

© John Deane

MRS. HENDERSON'S WINTER BREAKFAST

BREAKFAST PARTIES, ACCORDING TO MARY Henderson's 1876 *Practical Cooking and Dinner Giving*, were "less expensive than dinners, and just as satisfactory to guests." Don't schedule your breakfast as a modern *brunch*. "Guests might prefer to retain their strength by a repast at home if the breakfast-hour were at twelve o'clock, and then the fine breakfast would be less appreciated." She preferred nine or ten o'clock.

Broiled sardines on toast, garnished with
slices of lemon.
Tea, coffee, or chocolate.
Larded sweet-breads, garnished with French pease.
Cold French rolls or petit pains. Sauterne.
Small fillets or the tender cuts from
porter-house steaks,
served on little square slices of toast,
with mushrooms.
Fried oysters; breakfast puffs.
Fillets of grouse (each fillet cut in two) on little thin
slices of fried mush, garnished with potatoes
a la Parisienne.
Slices of oranges, with sugar.
Waffles, with maple syrup.

Kippers with a rack of stone-cold toast is popularly perceived as the quintessential British breakfast of expansive proportions.

Sardines on Toast

To some people, sardines are vulgar, but kippers are elegant and fashionably British. The function of both is the same—to awaken the palate and stimulate the thirst.

Until the 1880s the French monopolized sardine canning. It's likely that Mrs. Henderson in 1876 would have been using a French sardine fried and canned in olive oil, perhaps from Philippe et Canaud, the "oldest and largest-producing sardine-canning firm of Nantes," according to Elizabeth David. In 1962, she quoted one of the company's directors, "At an English meal I was given *hot* sardines, on cold toast. It was most strange. They were [our] sardines and I could not recognize them. The taste had become coarse. A little cayenne or lemon if you like. But, please, no shock treatment." Mrs. Henderson felt the English practice was more civilized obviously.

Sweetbreads

Sweetbreads with "French pease," according to Waverly Root's 1980 *Food,* is the classic French *ris de veau aux petit pois.* The best part of a veal thymus is the round or "heart sweetbread." He says this bland food seems light, but "they are rich and filling; a little of them goes a long way." He sautes his sweetbreads in half olive oil and half butter "with a whisper of chopped shallots and parsley." He accents his peas with "a sprig of thyme." Mrs. Henderson's *petit pois* probably came from a can. Root's observation about the camouflaged heartiness of sweetbreads could be applied to the whole of any Victorian multi-course meal. Many who read Victorian menus today assume that most Victorians consumed large helpings of each course; yet each was designed and served so "a little went a long way."

Waffles

The seventh course was not the main course of a twentieth-century breakfast, but the dessert course. Because the flavor of maple syrup is quite delicate, a bland wheat waffle won't overpower it. Victorians wouldn't make waffles at table because they didn't have electric waffle makers, but it would be fun to do so now. Dust the waffles with confectioners' sugar and pour on the syrup.

Beefsteaks

By the 1870s, especially in St. Louis where Mrs. Henderson lived, beefsteak was commonly served for substantial breakfasts in middle-class homes—"being always the same beefsteak, too frequently overcooked or undercooked, and often floating in butter." Its prevalence was due to the opening of Western grazing lands and the Victorian technologies of refrigeration and railroad transport. It was a Victorian "minute steak." In the French manner, Mrs. Henderson

© Stan Sholik/FPG International

Elevate waffles to elegance with the careful selection of ingredients, a variety of toppings, and a decorative setting. If the kiwi strikes a jarring contemporary note, substitute an orange, which would have been equally exotic to most Victorians.

elsewhere recommended sauces and garnishes, but her Winter Breakfast presents simple little steaks and mushrooms on toast.

As a substitute for beefsteak, Mrs. Henderson recommended little veal cutlets, actually small "escalopes." She took some lard, sauteed some slices of ham in it, reserved the ham, sauteed the tenderized and breaded

veal, removed the veal and used the remaining fat to make a sauce with flour, water, lemon juice, salt, and pepper. The veal was served with the sliced ham and sauce. Simple recipes, whether they are called schnitzel or *escalopes de veau* are best because they preserve the delicate flavor of the veal and maintain it as an elegant convenience food.

Fried Oysters

The fourth course was another Victorian fast food. Avoiding oysters from May through August was a useful fiction that gave over-harvested oyster beds a chance to recover. That, and being less liable to spoil in transit, is why they were favored during months whose names contained an "R." The "breakfast puffs" served with the oysters are leftover potatoes mashed with butter, eggs, and cream. "Pile it in rocky form on a dish; bake it in a quick oven until nicely colored. It will become quite light."

A breakfast nook can, with some ingenuity, be made decorative.

Les Restes

Anything sounds better said in French. *Les restes* is French for "left-overs." *Les restes* is what often appeared at the breakfast table for the main course. They were a previous evening's fish, meat, or fowl tranformed into hash, meatballs, potted meats, croquettes, sliced meat with sauce, or stew, i.e., something that didn't require carving.

It doesn't take prodigious talent to provide a good roast, but the economy of recycling left-overs into tasty dishes requires great skill. For leftover chicken, Mrs. Henderson liked Deviled Chicken with Cunard Sauce. Chopped chicken is broiled with butter and served with a one-two-three boiled sauce of one teaspoon (5 milliliters) prepared mustard, two tablespoons (30 milliliters) Worchestershire, and three tablespoons (45 milliliters) vinegar. "This dish is served on the Cunard steamers for supper. This makes a good winter breakfast."

Fillets of Grouse

The fifth course was prairie chicken. They took only fifteen to twenty minutes to roast, said Mrs. Henderson. But few of today's cooks, even if they could get them, have the patience to pluck them, store them until "well hung," and carve out the breasts after roasting. Waverly Root's *Food* says the flavor of young birds "is not improved by inviting them to rot" by hanging and calls it "lamentable snobbishness." Unless you can substitute another game bird, this part of the menu should be finessed. The fillets were served on fried leftover corn meal porridge or "mush." The potatoes à la Parisienne are little potato balls scooped out of raw potatoes and deep fat-fried in lard.

Sliced Oranges

The palate-cleansing oranges of the sixth course were probably tart, hence the need for added sugar. Glasses of orange juice, now commonly downed for breakfast, were considered a waste of expensive fruit during the Victorian period.

TEA FOR TWO

There is very little art in making good tea; if the water is boiling, and there is no sparing of the fragrant leaf, the beverage will almost invariably be good. The old-fashioned plan of allowing one teaspoonful [for each five and a half ounce cup], and one over, is still practised. Warm the teapot with boiling water; let it remain for two or three minutes for the vessel to become thoroughly hot, then pour it away. Put in the tea, pour in [about a cup] of boiling water, close the lid, and let it stand for the tea to draw from five to ten minutes; then fill [with the amount required. Remove the tea leaves before serving].

Isabella Beeton, *The Book of Household Management*, 1861

IF YOU CAN BOIL WATER, YOU CAN MAKE TEA. Think of the romantic surprise if the other half who doesn't usually cook suddenly makes something edible in the form of an intimate tea for two. Of all possible Victorian entertainments, tea for two requires the least effort and skill. Unlike other forms of tea, it is best impromptu. For intimacy, for romance, for true fellowship, it is the first choice of Victorian Lovers.

Some linens and porcelain can romanticize a corner of any room.

Mary Cassat's Five O'Clock Tea *of 1880 is a rare view of a Victorian lady actually drinking tea. The bold bars of the shrill wallpaper isolate and intensify the intimacy of the moment. These ladies say everything by saying nothing; this is the pleasure of company at its best.*

Tea Service

The only paraphernalia required for getting up or settling down in the bedroom is what Victorians called a "tête-à-tête" service of three pieces: teapot, sugar bowl, and cream pitcher. In the late nineteenth century, it was usually ceramic and often Japa-nese, especially after so many Americans had experienced the Japanese teahouse at the 1876 Centennial in Philadelphia's Fairmount Park.

Tête-à-tête services were also made in silver, like the one shown in Mary Cassatt's *Five O'Clock Tea*, which is minus the creamer because the two ladies are taking their tea only with sugar and not following the British custom of adding cream. Some may require lemon slices or a pot of special honey. Serving some imported tea biscuits, especially the famous English "digestive" biscuit, will require the addition of plates. There should also be a waste bowl for the tea bag, tea-ball infuser, or strained tea leaves that are removed from the pot before serving.

Teapot and teacups don't have to be the same pattern, but a splendidly decorated matching set is always a joy to behold.

Types of Tea

Tea varieties are as distinct as wine and can be appreciated in the same manner. There are dozens of teas, but here are seven of the most famous. Chinese Keemun, a black or fully fermented tea, is better known as *English Breakfast*. An aromatic afternoon tea blend scented with oil of bergamot is called *Earl Grey. Jasmine* is a delicate oolong or semifermented tea scented with jasmine flowers. *Formosa Oolong*, according to Schapira's solid and delightful 1975

Book of Coffee & Tea, is "the champagne of teas," "liquid sunshine," and "the philosopher's drink": "If you would but once savor the ambrosia that is a first rate Formosa Oolong, you would only share our horror at what constitutes tea in America today." *Gunpowder* is a green or unfermented tea made from young leaves rolled into small balls, hence its name, which has nothing to do with the strength of this delicate tea. *Darjeeling* is a hearty black tea grown on the slopes of the Himalayas.

Only make a single round because tea losses flavor rapidly. Extra cups should be made with fresh tea. Tea bags make tea as well as loose tea does, if the tea in the bag is as good as what you get loose and if you use them to brew tea in the pot instead of the cup. According to Schapira, the tea bag was invented by a New York coffee and tea merchant named Thomas Sullivan in 1904.

After that incident in Boston Harbor in the late eighteenth century, consumption of tea in the United States suffered from lingering Victorian associations with Britain, aristocracy, and ladies. Then Yankee Clip-

A COMPROMISE.
He: "SEAL BRAND COFFEE leads the rest"
She: "ROYAL GEM TEA BRAND is best"
He: "Still we need not disagree"
    "Mine's best coffee; your's best tea"
She: "thus to fix it I'm not loath
    Since CHASE AND SANBORN import them both."

"We've got to stop meeting like this" reveals the Victorian gender bias about coffee for men and tea for women. The flip side of this card echoes it with a functional, straight-sided coffee pot and plain coffee cup for him, a beautiful, oriental teapot and decorated teacup for her.

per ships of the 1850s and 1860s ended British domination of the China Trade and transformed tea into a beverage anyone could afford. Because tea was most often served in the home when men were at work, it continued to be considered as a ladies' drink, an association strengthened in the late nineteenth century by public tearooms and cafes that were instantly successful because they were the first socially acceptable places ladies could refresh themselves without male escorts.

© Jim Krajicek

My love for thine.

Victorian gender bias about tea survives today, especially when it is served with trimmed and triangled sandwiches. This is a stereotypical ladies' tea.

Spring

MAY DAY BREAKFAST

THE FIRST OF MAY
With bang and crash and clatter-clat,
With carmen bawling "Hey! hey!"
With broken china, stoven hat,
My children missing—Loo and Mat—
It comes, the dreaded May-day.

Augustus Comstock, 1867

VICTORIAN MAY DAY WAS CITY CHAOS AND country celebration. May Day in the city was a grim form of musical chairs called Moving Day. Streets looked like shipwrecks with furniture and other cargo bumping and bobbing like flotsam, moved by carters at exorbitant rates. May Day in the country was "going a-Maying" with a sunrise walk, eating a May Day Breakfast, crowning the Queen of the May, and dancing around a Maypole. May Day was the Spring equivalent of Thanksgiving Harvest Festival and second only to Christmas in popularity.

Any of your Victoriana-loving friends will probably enjoy helping you adorn your period house in the appropriate colors. Note, however, that next May Day they will undoubtedly expect the favor paid back in kind.

A NATURE WALK

To honor these traditions, you might organize a reception to welcome a newcomer to your neighborhood. Or form a work party to help a new Victorian Lover with an old house or apartment. Or make a breakfast to celebrate good flowers, good friends, and good surroundings. Fill a small basket with flowers or make a paper basket from strips of brown poster-board and fill it with tissue paper flowers. Tie the invitation card to the handle and hang one on each guest's front door.

If your group is composed of ardent Druids, you might assemble in the wee hour before sunrise. Most people would trade the pleasures of sunrise for an early morning walk. Serve a simple eye-opener of coffee or tea and some biscuits at the assembly point. To establish the hour of breakfast, time the walk in advance and make it proceed without delays.

BREAKFAST

May Day perambulation justifies a substantial breakfast presented in courses. Serve the breakfast buffet-style if necessary, though after a brisk walk most guests will appreciate a place to sit down. Start with an orange or grapefruit cut and sectioned basket-style with a small flower tied to the handle. Follow with creamed codfish on toast, and end with a savory course of curried eggs. You might substitute creamed dried-beef for the dried cod, and May Day devilled egg salad for the curried eggs. An easier but equally appropriate salad is lettuce and watercress dressed with mayonnaise. A special Spring treat is broiled frog's legs, but baked beans with Boston brown bread is easier and was more common in the Victorian era. If a selection of jams, jellies, and honeys served with bland crackers or more toast is not enough for sweet tooths, you might serve a dessert course of waffles with fancy toppings.

Sally Lunn, or an approximation of it, is an appropriate cake for a May Day Breakfast.

After a trudge through the landscape, most people will prefer to sit down to your breakfast rather than stand before a buffet.

Sally Lunn

A popular Victorian breakfast cake was Sally Lunn, a French sun and moon cake, or *soleil lune*. Making this yeast cake is so complicated relative to the results that a subterfuge is in order. Elizabeth David's 1980 *English Bread and Yeast Cookery* describes Sally Lunn as a "kind of brioche-type cake—or perhaps a better description would be an extra-light leavened Victorian sponge cake." If you can buy a brioche, christen it Sally Lunn with a baptism of sugar and milk glaze. It's very British to eat it with a thick cream that has been scalded and clotted, but the cake tends to lose and the cream win. Elizabeth David prefers her cake straight. In place of waffles, you might move the orange or grapefruit baskets to the end of the meal and serve them with slices of Sally Lunn.

May Day is the occasion for home-grown flowers.

Flowers and the May Pole

Decorate the May Day dining room with blossoms. Yards usually benefit from some thinning of the flowering shrubs and trees. If you have any bulbs in bloom that need dividing, dig them up, put them in decorative containers for May Day Breakfast, and then divide them prior to replanting. A favorite Victorian conceit was transforming the table into a garden with formal beds of colorful food displayed between the flowers and vines.

Dancing around the Maypole was an ancient Rite of Spring performed at Victorian women's colleges as late as the 1950s, likewise at elementary schools with little girls dressed as fairies. Today the proper place for a Maypole is a table centerpiece. Use a mailing tube, securely attaching it to a broad, flat base and topping it with a ball. Wind the cylinder with col-

Floral code was a popular Victorian form of non-verbal communication. It has dwindled today into the single love message of a dozen red roses.

ored ribbons that fan out at the base and terminate at place cards or favor baskets with floral decorations.

Appropriate party favors would be packets of flower seeds. They symbolize the Victorian passion for floral decorations of all kinds, not only in their gardens but in their carpets, ceramics, needlework, draperies, dresses, and wallpapers. Take the occasion to explore the Victorian Language of Flowers that associated messages and emotions with various flowers. Compose something with the flowers at hand and ask the company to decode it, or buy some old floral postcards and try to decipher them.

Along with the revival of Victorian gardens for Victorian homes, there has grown a suspicion that something good from the past has been lost; hence the effort to preserve and propagate antique varieties of roses, especially those that are fragrant. The May Day Breakfast might be used to focus attention on reviving these lost but not forgotten flowers.

"This same party," in the delicate words of *The Calendar of Entertainments*, "could be adapted to an afternoon and evening affair if one's guests are not ardent enough nature lovers to rise so early." By the 1920s, when this was published, the luxury of rising at midday, characteristic of Victorian landed gentry and their country-house guests, had spread downwards in the social scale. If your friends are in the habit of going to bed with the moon instead of rising with the sun, the May Day program of exercise, eating, and edification can be as profitably carried out after noon as before it.

DECORATION DAY PICNIC

Hand coloring by Melissa Dehncke

Victorian rural cemeteries were places of veneration, beauty, and public assembly. This Harper's Weekly engraving of May 31, 1867 shows Virginians at Richmond celebrating Decoration Day in their Hollywood Cemetery before the event was appropriated by the Union Army. Hollywood was designed by Philadelphia architect John Notman in 1848.

The beat of the band had put life into the wavering marching columns, even into the Civil War Veterans. The sight of that uneven marching company took Melville's breath away, and before he knew it he found himself on the street following the parade with other boys from Nashua. The band was like the flute of the Pied Piper playing its tune to childhood. He would have followed the band anywhere and perhaps that band was playing for him still.

John P. Marquand, *Melville Goodwin*, 1951.

DECORATION DAY WAS VICTORIAN CIVIL WAR Memorial Day. In the last 125 years, the focus of Memorial Day has been changed, although in some parts of the South it is Confederacy Day. Despite twentieth century efforts to transform the holiday into a memorial for all United States wars and veterans, for most Americans it is the end of spring and the beginning of summer vacation.

If one of the functions of Victorian entertaining is to provide opportunities for better understanding our history, a Decoration Day picnic can be rich with rewards if you and your friends approach it with open eyes and minds.

A TRIP TO THE CEMETERY

The main barrier between you and the Victorians isn't their heroic attitude towards war; it's their romance with death, beautifully embodied in Victorian Rural Cemeteries. It may strike you as grotesque or even obscene that Victorians used rural cemeteries as public pleasure grounds, even picnicking within their family plots. These "Cities of the Dead," as Victorians proudly called them, were prototypes for cities of the living. Today's American Dream of urban parks and parklike suburban residential developments owe their origins to Victorian rural cemeteries of which the first—Mount Auburn in Cambridge founded in 1829 overlooking the Charles River—is the most beautiful.

If you have any affection for the visual remains of the Victorian Era, the best open-air museums are the Victorian rural cemeteries. They are filled with mature plantings of favorite Victorian trees and shrubs. They have yards of decorative cast-iron fences and gates and dozens of cast-iron seats. The sculpture is always interesting, sometimes splendid. The tombs are always eye-catching, sometimes bizarre. On a splendid day, Victorian cemeteries have a beauty and serenity—a romantic hush—unlike any other place.

Many of these rural cemeteries need "friends" to help with their preservation as outdoor museums of Victoriana. Any public recognition that a sensitively organized Decoration Day picnic might bring to the existence and plight of these Victorian treasures would probably be welcomed by the management. Cash to help maintain the perimeter walls and fences, gateways, and roads also would be welcome; so would tidying up a selected area to whet appetites for the picnic fare. A tour might be arranged featuring some of the most interesting monuments. Brief histories of some of the more illustrious residents might be assigned and read out during the tour.

© John Crosby Freeman

For wealthy Victorians it was "in life so in death." In rural cemeteries like Philadelphia's Laurel Hill overlooking the Schuylkill River, designed by John Notman in 1836, they took the hill sites, got the best views, and built the biggest houses. These sections are a microcosm of Victorian architectural revivals.

BILL OF FARE FOR A PICNIC FOR FORTY PERSONS

The following appears to be the standard Victorian multi-course meal moved outdoors—dinner alfresco. The clue is not the pile of meats but the baskets of beverages: begin with the sherry, serve the claret with the meats, champagne with the desserts, and finish with the brandy. The thirty-six quarts of ale and seventy-two bottles of ginger-beer, soda-water, and lemonade were mostly for priors and afters. We, victimized by our polluted waterways, can only contemplate with envy Mrs. Beeton's final advice: "Water can usually be obtained, so it is useless to take it."

A joint of cold roast beef, a joint of cold boiled beef, two ribs of lamb, two shoulders of lamb, four roast fowls, two roast ducks, one ham, one tongue, two veal-and-ham pies, two pigeon pies, six medium-size lobsters, one piece of collared calf's head, eighteen lettuces, six baskets of salad, six cucumbers. Stewed fruit well sweetened, three or four dozen plain pastry biscuits to eat with the stewed fruit, two dozen fruit turnovers, four dozen cheesecakes, two cold puddings in moulds, two blanc-manges in moulds, a few jam puffs, one large cold plum pudding, a few baskets of fresh fruit, three dozen plain biscuits, a piece of cheese, six pounds of butter, assorted breads, rolls, and cakes, one half pound of tea. Coffee is not suitable for a picnic, being difficult to make.

Just as today's RVs assault nature with modern conveniences and technology, wealthy Victorians also made few concessions to the reality of the woods with splendid spreads like these.

© Chas Schneider/FPG International

Things not to be forgotten at a Picnic

A stick of horseradish, bottles of mint-sauce, salad dressing, vinegar, and made mustard, pepper, salt, good oil, and pounded sugar. If it can be managed, take a little ice. It is scarcely necessary to say that plates, tumblers, wine glasses, knives, forks, and spoons, must not be forgotten; as also tea cups and saucers, three or four teapots, some lump sugar, and milk, if this last-named article cannot be obtained in the neighborhood. Take three corkscrews.

Beverages—three dozen quart bottles of ale, packed in hampers; ginger-beer, soda-water, and lemonade, of each two dozen bottles; six bottles of sherry, six bottles of claret, champagne a discretion, and any other light wine that may be preferred, and two bottles of brandy.

Isabella Beeton,
Book of Household Management, 1861

ARBOR DAY
GARDEN PARTY LUNCHEON

There are trees (like those women, who, though brilliant in drawing-rooms, are never less than ladies when busy in domestic labors) which are useful and profitable in orchard and forest, are doubly beautiful in robes of greater luxuriance upon the carpet of a rich lawn. There are others which no care in culture will make ornaments in "the best society."

Frank J. Scott, *The Art of Beautifying Suburban Home Grounds*, 1886

TREE-PLANTING IS ANOTHER ASPECT OF Victorian individual responsibility that has gone out of fashion in the late twentieth century. It deserves to be revived along with Arbor Day, a Victorian celebration that began in Nebraska on April 10, 1872. On Northern calendars it usually appears on the last Friday in April; on Southern calendars it appears from December through February. From 1882 until well into the twentieth century it was a popular school festival. Perhaps it still is in some sections.

Arbor Day continues to be promoted by the National Arbor Day Foundation as part of a broad-based conservation effort. You might join this non-profit organization and then ask them for entertaining ideas. Or you might use the occasion to study and revive Victorian shrubs and trees in particular and Victorian landscaping styles in general. Forest conservation, along with the protection of natural areas like Yellowstone, was a great Victorian achievement. You might celebrate this by a picnic in a nearby forest.

Late Victorian suburbanites upholstered their landscapes with the same enthusiasm with which they upholstered their parlors.

56

Hand coloring by Melissa Dehncke

ROBINSON & C? BRISTOL

Victorians tended to regard the grounds surrounding their homes as extensions of their interior spaces; hence a garden party, like the one shown in this stock British printer's cut, was merely an indoor party moved out-of-doors. They dressed as if nothing was different. They look uncomfortable; they probably were. Today, one would be ill-advised to turn a Victorian garden party into a costume ball. Simple, flowing, light-colored clothes with picture hats and straw boaters would be more practical.

PLANTING TREES

Trees increase the value of municipal as well as individual real estate. As part of a revived commitment to neighborhood and community by urban pioneers and Victorian Lovers in historic districts, an Arbor Day celebration is an easy and economical way to improve the environment by the planting of trees. If your community suffers from limited public funds, it might welcome such an improvement at no public expense. If turned into a media event, tools and trees might be donated in return for favorable publicity.

Courtesy Motif Designs

Courtesy Laura Ashley

Your organization's reward for its work is a garden party luncheon either in the newly planted area or a member's garden. Served buffet-style, there are several possible menus. It could be light—what used to be called "ladies' lunch"—or it could be quite substantial. It could be like a tea or a dessert, depending on the relationship of beverages to cakes. If the party is located on public property, it would be prudent to avoid alcoholic beverages. On private property, you have a glorious opportunity to explore two Victorian forms of tipple called *punch* and *cup*.

Victorian garden parties don't require special furniture. Even the most industrial-strength tables can be gracefully covered with large cloths that reach the ground; folding chairs can be bagged with unbleached muslin and pretty ribbons or bedecked with pillows. The garden is the focal objet d'art; *anything else will be secondary.*

Punch and Cup

Here are recipes for punch and cup taken from an Edwardian recipe book published in New York by Meriden Silversmiths. The punch recipe is that old mainstay of the Philadelphia arsenal, Fish House Punch. Its evil heart of peach brandy tricks neophytes into thinking that something tasting so good can't possibly do a body any harm. It can... and it will.

Old recipes will make sense if you remember that a *pony* equals one ounce (thirty milliliters), a *jigger* equals one-and-a-half ounces (forty five milliliters), and a *gill* equals one quarter pint, four ounces, or one-half cup (120 milliliters).

Philadelphia Fish House Punch

Three-fourths of a pound of white sugar dissolved in water, one-third of a pint of lemon juice, one-half of a pint of Cognac, one-fourth of a pint of Peach Brandy, one-fourth of a pint of Jamaica Rum, and one quart of Apollinaris, with large lump of ice in bowl.

To make it less sweet and easier to mix, use one half pound (.23 kilogram) of powdered sugar. Use a quart of domestic club soda instead of the imported Apollinaris. Squeeze six lemons for the juice.

Various containers of Victorian vintage or style will put your table into bloom, whether it is located on the verandah or indoors.

Baskets and colorful linens are simple, but evocative design elements.

Champagne Cup

Two ponies of Cognac, two ponies of white Curaçao, two ponies of Maraschino, two lemons, one quart Champagne, one bottle Club Soda, cucumber-rind, berries in season; sugar to taste, four or five sprigs of mint, one large lump of ice.

This is the beverage described by Edith Wharton in her 1923 story about the 1840s titled *False Dawn:* "Hay, verbena and mignonette scented the languid day. Large strawberries, crimsoning through sprigs of mint floated in a bowl of pale yellow cup on the verandah table."

Claret Cup

Same as above, but add two ponies of Benedictine and two Curaçao, instead of white Cognac and Curaçao, and use Claret instead of Champagne.

Rhine-Wine Or Sauterne Cup

Same as Champagne Cup, but add Rhine Wine or Sauterne instead of Champagne.

At a later time, when local strawberries are available, you might try Claret Cup à la Willard's, taken from Charles Ranhofer's *The Epicurean*, 1893. To the basic recipe of a pint of claret sweetened to taste and one half cup (120 mililiters) of maraschino or Curaçao add one pound (one half kilogram) crushed strawberries, the juice of one lemon, and four teaspoons (twenty grams) powdered sugar. Dilute with a bottle of chilled club soda or seltzer water, and serve topped with whipped cream.

LITTLE GIRLS' TEA PARTY

So now for a feast,
Bread and jam at the least,
And there's cake on a dish
For those who may wish;
Milk and water and sugar and very weak tea.

Eliza Keary, *At Home Again*, 1883

This lovely scene of little girls enjoying an Oriental tea was actually an advertisement for O + O Tea: notice the logo placed unobtrusively in the light fixture.

NURSERY TEA, A FANTASY ENTERTAINMENT played out with dolls and a miniature tea service by children born into wealthy families, was a Victorian tradition continued from Georgian times.

FANCIFUL FASHIONS IN A GARDEN SETTING

The best Victorian entertainment for little girls is a tea party held on the verandah or in the garden. Dress the girls in Victorian Revival fashions. This will delight their parents and make the girls feel special. Holding the party outdoors will reduce parental anxiety about spills.

Encourage the girls to participate in all aspects of the entertainment from making up the guest list and sending out the invitations to cleaning up afterwards. "Cakes" are easily made from common white bread shaped with favorite cookie cutters and layered with jams or jellies. If adults are attending and you want to bake something Victorian but

Our earliest memories should be like teddy bears—soft, warm, and comforting. Your little girls might like to invite their bears to the tea party.

simple enough for the children to make, consider "Victoria Sandwiches"—a kind of sponge cake leavened with eggs, cut into fingers, and layered with jam or marmalade.

Set the tea table as grand or as simple as you like, consulting the girls as much as possible. If you put an old colored bedsheet over a card table, you will be entertaining in a Late Victorian tradition known as Color Teas, named for the dominant color of the table decor. Your old sheet then becomes the basis for a harmonious collection of colored cloth or paper napkins, serving dishes, the floral arrangement, and even the tea service itself. It is easier to arrange a Color Tea for adults or girls outdoors than inside because it does not have to be adapted to the existing parlor or dining room decor. At the other extreme, tea can be served on a bare wicker table. Paper or crocheted doilies would be an attractive alternative to fancy linen.

Tea and Tea Leaves

The girls can be given various kinds of "tea": sugar, milk, and water; weak tea and warm milk; or one of the herbal teas, perhaps an apple spice. Any liquid given to children should be warm, not hot.

You may offer the girls several different kinds of tea. When they've finished a cup, they may enjoy "reading the tea leaves."

Although one of the advantages of an adult tea is that service plates are not required because the food is bite-size and hand-held, children will require plates. Young girls will probably be more comfortable with children's tea cups. New or old, they should be substantial to resist breakage. Older girls should be introduced to adult porcelain, for how can they learn to appreciate fine things if they are not given the chance?

A tea for young girls might end with a session of making pictures with tea leaves. Make them drink all of their tea, then spoon some wet leaves into each emptied cup. Swirl or arrange with a teaspoon an interesting shape on the bottom of each cup, including one of your own. Peer into your cup, tell the girls what you see,

and ask them if they see the same picture. That should get them started on their own cups. You might leave them with the following advice provided by C.C. Ward in "Tea-Cup Lore" in an 1884 issue of *St. Nicholas Magazine*: "The pictures can be made all black, like a silhouette, or they can be white in parts, by removing all of the sediment, and leaving the white of the cup for faces, hands or other parts of the picture." Don't feel guilty if you take this children's game back to your adult tea table. A tea for older girls might end with "reading the tea leaves."

A simple apron and hair ribbon can Victorianize any little girl. High button shoes are not obligatory.

Victoria Sandwiches

INGREDIENTS—four eggs; their weight in pounded sugar, butter, and flour; a pinch of salt, a layer of any kind of jam or marmalade.

Mode—*Beat the butter to a cream; dredge [i.e, mix] in the flour and pounded sugar; stir these ingredients well together, and add the eggs, which should be previously thoroughly whisked. When the mixture has been well beaten for about ten minutes, butter a [pan], pour in the batter, and bake it in a moderate oven for twenty minutes. Let it cool, spread one half of the cake with a layer of nice preserve, place over it the other half of the cake, press the pieces slightly together, and then cut it into long finger-pieces; pile them in cross-bars on a glass dish, and serve. Sufficient for five or six persons.*

Isabella Beeton,
Book of Household Management, 1861

If you mix the cake in a food processor, it will reduce the preparation time and mess potential of youthful helpers, but the chance to use up their surplus energy by stirring will be lost. Ditto the substitution of confectioners' sugar denying the children the satisfaction of pounding regular sugar in a large plastic storage bag with the flat side of a wooden meat tenderizer or a rubber mallet. A moderate oven is 350 degrees F (175 degrees C).

© Courtesy R. Twining & Company Ltd

Slices of cake sandwiched by superb preserves are raised to the peerage when called Victoria Sandwiches. A cloth with decorations reminiscent of a Gothic Revival encaustic tiled floor adds to the illusion.

QUEEN VICTORIA'S BIRTHDAY HIGH TEA

It is no disgrace for any civilized people to honor her by celebrating her natal day, whatever their political government, and it is with pride and pleasure that I propose: "Queen Victoria—Sovereign, Wife and Mother— Long may she reign!"

Hill's Manual of Social & Business Forms, 1884

This lovely statue is of Queen Victoria as a young girl.

QUEEN VICTORIA'S BIRTHDAY IS THE OCCASION for a grand Victorian tea party anywhere. In Canada and the U.K., it's a legal holiday celebrated on the first Monday before May 25. In the U.S., it can be a celebration of a great Victorian woman. Call it "High Tea" to elevate the event and raise expectations about the food. Time it as a luncheon, supper, buffet, or dessert party. Locate it inside, on a verandah, on a lawn, or in a garden. Offer a variety of meat, fish, vegetable, and cheese sandwiches, fresh fruits, and pretty cakes. Decorate with lace and rich "royal" colors of blue, purple, or red. Fold the napkins into crowns.

© Peter Paige: Design by Easton & LaRocca

Queen Victoria's birthday party can be made festive by decorating with elegantly wrapped packages and other decorations in "royal" colors like purple and red. An empty armchair in honor of Her Majesty might be draped with a bit of ermine or another fur.

© Robert Perron

HOUSE TOUR

Organize a tour of one special house in your town or several. Explore inside and out, including the garden.

If you make the Queen's Birthday into a neighborhood or community celebration for Victorian Lovers, consider doing what the Van Wyck Brooks Historic District in Plainfield, New Jersey, did in 1985. They organized a fund-raising historic house tour that ended in a garden party behind one of the houses, the high point of which was Battenburg Cake Contest. Six entries were entered, judged, and eaten.

TEA DELICACIES

Victorian cookbooks assumed their readers didn't need to be told how to make sandwiches; that's why they have so few recipes for them. If you need help, you will find it in Edwardian cookbooks and specialized sandwich guides of the 1910s and 1920s.

Meat sandwiches are the classic addition made to distinguish "high tea" from "low," but cakes are what your guests will remember. Little iced cakes piled on plates or pedestals into pyramids or arranged in cake baskets are the cornerstones of the formal tea table. Treat your guests to cakes easily made from scratch with the finest ingredients you can find.

A pyramid of assorted cakes will be more immediately attractive and give more satisfaction than an elaborately ornamented cake on which two to three days' work has been put.

Jessup Whitehead, *The Steward's Handbook*, 1893

Whitehead, a Chicago-based publisher to the Late Victorian hotel trade, provides the following trade secrets about party cakes. Thin sheet cakes are more practical than thick layer cakes. Make an assortment of white, yellow, and chocolate sheet cakes. Layer some sheets with jams and jellies that haven't been overwhelmed with sugar. Leave some plain "for those who prefer it." Glaze the remaining sheets with wet confectioner's sugar "so thick that it will just barely settle down smooth and glossy when poured; it will dry in an hour [and] not break, but can be cut into any fancy shape that the cake will bear." Wet the sugar with water, egg yolks, or chocolate syrup for three basic colors. Or use natural dyes like beet juice, fruit syrup, wine, or spirits. Or scatter finely chopped citron, coconut, or nuts on the glazed cakes before they dry. "Let the flavors be various; almond, pineapple, orange, vanilla, banana, lemon, anise, peppermint, peach."

Courtesy R. Twinings & Company Ltd.

Tiers of little iced cakes never fail to delight the eye, stimulate hunger, and elevate an event. If the porcelain is pretty, so much the better.

Battenburg Cake

The proper confection for Queen Victoria's Birthday Party is Battenburg Cake covered with delicious almond paste. Sometimes fancifully decorated, it's more of a memorial to the famous marzipan of Prince Albert's North German homeland than to Queen Victoria. The cake combines equal weights of butter, sugar, and flour; the number of eggs are half that weight expressed in ounces; teaspoons of baking powder are half again. For example: eight ounces (224 grams) of butter, sugar, and flour will require four eggs and two teaspoons (10 milliliters) baking powder. Add some vanilla extract for flavor. If it needs extra moisture, add some milk. If you don't want to experiment, your favorite yellow cake recipe will do just as well.

Instead of stripes, a checkerboard composition is used for the classic Battenburg Cake served at The Queen Victoria Inn's birthday party in Cape May, New Jersey.

On her birthday, think of Queen Victoria as she was on her coronation day in her robes of state, as captured by Winterhalter.

Divide the batter evenly into two bowls and color one of them with cocoa or chocolate syrup. Pour each bowl of batter into an oblong loaf pan. Bake at 375 degrees F (190 degrees C) for twenty-five minutes, then let cool. Cut the cakes in half lengthwise and cement the four pieces into a four layer striped loaf with apricot or raspberry jam.

Make the almond paste from your favorite recipe, or buy some ready-made in a can. Like pie dough, roll out the marzipan using regular sugar instead of flour to keep it from sticking. Cut out the squares and rectangles required to encase the cake. After hardening them in the refrigerator for a few hours, cement them to the cake with jam. Join the edges by piping on some icing in a different color with a pastry bag. If you're an expert in this department, you could add your own marzipan decorations, but most people will preserve their sanity by purchasing the animals and other ornaments from their local fancy baker.

Beaten by Battenburg before you begin? Queen Victoria had a passion for cherries—another famous product of Prince Albert's homeland. According to Iris Frey's 1982 *Crumpets and Scones*, Queen Victoria specified a cherry tart for her coronation banquet "and had second helpings lavishly topped with whipped cream." Any cake or tart with cherries would do honor to Her Majesty. Making them bite-size is convenient for a stand-up affair and allows one to do without plates.

Crumpets and Jam

High Tea wouldn't be complete without crumpets soaked in melted butter and covered with jam. As Mrs. Beeton pointed out in *Household Management*, there isn't much difference between English muffins and crumpets. Both are small, round yeast breads baked on a griddle, and toasted before eating. "To every quart of milk allow one and a half ounces (45 milliliters) yeast, a little salt; flour." Muffin dough is divided and rounded into shape with the hands after the first rising and evenly baked on both sides after the second rising. Crumpet batter is given one rising, poured into round metal forms on the griddle, baked on the first side until the famous "nooks" bubble out on the surface, and briefly baked on the other side. When done, they resemble a limp, half-baked pancake.

Both of these griddle breads were Victorian teatime favorites. They didn't require men or servants to slice them. They didn't crumble or disintegrate when held in the hand like regular bread. Best of all, they were elegant sponges for butter and jam. A word of caution, however, about crumpets: inspect the bottom before you slather on the good stuff; they have the embarrassing potential of taking it in at the top and releasing it through the bottom!

Like kippers for breakfast, crumpets for tea are regarded as typically British upper crust. Unlike kippers, they are inexpensive and can be made at home. It's a good idea to remove the tea ball after the brewing period; it may be beautiful in itself, but no sensible person will let it drain unto their saucer.

KENTUCKY DERBY BUFFET

*Nowhere is there produced so colorable a picture of what
the Old South must have been as Derby Day;
it recreates and revives a simulation of a phase of life
which elsewhere practically has vanished;
here is one spot where for one day the spirit of commercialism
runs second to the spirit of an Olden Time.*

Irvin S. Cobb, *Kentucky*, 1924

*This illustration from a Currier and Ives calendar depicts a typical day at the races. These horses, with chariots in place, are getting ready
for the "Trot."*

THE KENTUCKY DERBY IS NOT NORTH AMERICA'S oldest surviving annual horse race; that honor belongs to the Queen's Plate in Toronto, Canada endowed by King William IV in 1836. But the "run for the roses" at Churchill Downs in Louisville is North America's most famous annual horse race. Prior to the 1930s, The Derby was homage to Kentucky's position as the world's biggest producer of thoroughbred horses. The Derby was also a "coming-out party" for debutantes. That, and its pre-Prohibition supply of bourbon, gave truth to the old Kentucky boast about its "good-looking women, fine whiskey, and fast horses."

Courtesy New York Public Library

A History of Entertainments

The bloodlines of thoroughbred racing in Victorian America are thoroughly British. Diomed, the winner of the first Epsom Derby in 1780, was one of four Derby winners imported into the United States between 1783 and 1800 along with scores of other stallions. In the nineteenth century, Epsom was an ancient course, founded during the reign of James I, but Ascot, founded by Queen Anne near Windsor castle early in the eighteenth century, was the most fashionable British racing event.

The first Kentucky Derby ran May 17, 1875; today the first "leg" of the "Triple Crown" is run the first Saturday in May. The other legs also date from Victorian times: The Preakness in Baltimore, Maryland was first run in 1873 and the Belmont Stakes, on Long Island in 1867. After the

Civil War, American races were shortened from series of four-mile (6.4 kilometers) "heats" to a single heat in the English "classic" distance of one and a half (2.4 kilometers) miles. This was the Kentucky Derby standard until 1896, when it was shortened to one and a quarter miles (2 kilometers). The classic distance still survives at the Belmont Stakes.

The weight system of handicapping was established in New York in 1873 by the formation of the Jockey Club, modelled after its English counterpart. Bookmaking was imported from England in the 1870s, along with French *pari-mutuel* wagering. The trotter as a breed begins with the publication in 1871 of the *American Trotting Register*. The Grand Circuit of harness racing dates to 1873.

These are a few of the highlights of horse racing's fascinating Victorian background that justify a special Victorian entertainment in its honor. Folks in Louisville party for a week, unconsciously perpetuating Victorian entertainments like a big parade, Fillies Ball, and steamboat race between *The Belle of Louisville* and *The Delta Queen*, its archrival from Cincinnati.

THE PICNIC

Derby Day buffets are located according to the weather: inside, on the verandah, or in the garden. They usually feature beaten biscuits and thinly sliced country ham. So important is country ham as a symbol of the Old South on Derby Day that a conference was held in its honor prior to Derby Week in 1988.

© D. Spindel/FPG International

Country Ham

The significance of country ham isn't regional; it's international. Americans may justifiably claim the turkey as their own. The coastal areas all over the world may celebrate their seafood. Some people may even acquiesce to fast-food burgers and fried chicken as remarkably American. But the pig has meant more to the Americans than any other animal. Unlike chickens, sheep, and cattle raised chiefly for their eggs, wool, and milk, swine were raised solely for their meat. They were prolific, productive, low maintenance livestock that thrived on scraps. Early in the nineteenth century, packers at Cincinnati invented the integrated assembly-line production system which, it was said, used everything "except the curl in its tail." This won Cincinnati the Victorian nickname of "Porkopolis."

However, Queen Victoria was fond of country ham, ordering quantities of the famous peanut-fed Smithfield hams of Virginia. Today's connoisseurs allege significant differences between regions, producers, feed, and breed, but more important is the quality of the ham, the care with which it is cured and smoked, and the length of time it is hung before eating. Kentucky aficionados prefer salt-cured ham that has gone through a "June sweat," i.e., an autumn ham left in the smokehouse to naturally freeze in the winter and "sweat" in the summer. American writing about American food is forced by American cultural inferiority to describe something really good such as country ham as

the American equivalent of something European. Hence country ham is often described as "American prosciutto." Mrs. Henderson bitterly complained in 1876 about this willful self-deprecation in her *Practical Cooking*, remarking that American cheeses were being "exported in immense quantities to England, where they are considered by epicures as great luxuries." The best, she said, was made in Otsego County, New York, but it was exported as "English dairy" cheese. "Why do they not call it Otsego cheese?" she wailed.

Mint Julep

Salty country ham makes people thirsty, which brings us to the sainted Mint Julep, subject of much good-natured cajolery. The classic remark is credited to World War II hero General Simon Bolivar Buckner, who declared, "[Making a julep] is a rite that must not be trusted to a novice, a statistician nor a Yankee." This and other interesting memorabilia can be found in Richard Barksdale Harwell's delightful slim volume *The Mint Julep*, published by the University Press of Virginia in 1975.

The essentials for the perfect julep are a glass, tumbler, or goblet filled with crushed ice and bourbon whiskey flavored by a minted sugar syrup. A silver vessel enhances surface condensation. A sprig of mint stuck in the top aids the aesthetic as well as delivers aroma to the olfactories. Excess sugar must be avoided. For more information, consult *The Mint Julep.* Even dedicated bourbon drinkers usually can't tolerate more than one of these sweet drinks. Instead, they settle down happily with "bourbon and branch," i.e., whisky and water, for the rest of the day.

Bourbon Cake

Another way to celebrate corn whiskey during Derby Day is Bourbon Cake, a nut-raisin cake sprinkled and brushed with some bourbon after it has cooled. A recipe can be found in James Beard's *American Cookery* (1972), which he calls "Whiskey, Moonshine, or Feuding Cake." Using spirits in this way is an old and frugal method of reviving stale cakes and extending the life of fresh ones. The most popular Victorian version was Tipsy Cake made from stale sponge cake soaked with sherry instead of bourbon and covered with custard. You can make any cake "tipsy" and name it for the moistening spirit by sprinkling, brushing, or soaking.

To further celebrate corn (the main ingredient of bourbon) as another of America's food contribution to the world in your Derby Day buffet, consider corn muffins, fritters, pone, hoecake, dodgers, johnnycake, or hush puppies. Recipes for many of them are in standard cookbooks. All of them have their devotees. One dissenter is *The Joy of Cooking,* commenting on the folklore of deep-fried corn bread thrown by fishermen to their dogs with the cry "Hush! Puppy"—"Maybe this is still the best use for them."

The essence of a Kentucky Derby Buffet is common things done uncommonly well; for what is more common than ham, bourbon, fried chicken, and cake? But for those who care more about food that tastes good than food in good taste, it is an honorable meal that requires no apology.

The Buffet Table

Rent or borrow horse-racing paraphernalia to decorate your buffet. Some library research will reveal the owner's "silks" of Derby horses, which could be used to match guests by cutting swatches in half and having them draw their partners from a saddle bag. They would then be obliged to cheer that horse from the gate to the wire. White suits for gentlemen and picture hats for ladies might be encouraged.

Derby Day buffet is a Victorian entertainment that could be run several times during the racing season. If you want to celebrate the races at Saratoga, add to your buffet that great Victorian contribution to American cuisine—Saratoga Potatoes, better known as potato chips.

Fried Chicken and Potatoes Kentucky Style

An alternative to country ham is Kentucky Fried Chicken, if you can overlook its tarnished, fast-food name. Revive its honor with authenticity. Coat it with cornmeal and fry it in lard. Serve it with "Potatoes in Kentucky Style," which the 1881 *Buckeye Cooking & Practical Housekeeping* revealed as good old scalloped potatoes. Today, some Louisville Derby Day buffets substitute sliced eggs for the potatoes and cracker crumbs for the flour.

Summer

WHEELMEN'S VERANDAH BREAKFAST

Serving oatmeal *"as a first course enables the cook to prepare many dishes, such as steaks, omelets, etc., just as the family sit down to breakfast; and when the porridge is eaten, she is ready with the other dishes 'smoking hot.'"*

Mary Henderson,
Practical Cooking and Dinner Giving, 1876

© Jeff McNamara

A BICYCLE TOUR

"WHEELMEN" IS A LATE VICTORIAN TERM that included ladies; they often had their own cycling clubs. Ladies peddled around in loose, ladylike garb suitable to the season, but gentlemen usually wore skintight pants and shirts, especially when in competition. The effect of this was not lost on the ladies who idolized the most famous male cyclists into Victorian versions of beefcake pinups. When cycling in mixed company, male cycling attire was less suggestive and flirtation become more verbal. Cycling in any form was justified by the Victorian worship of Nature, which is what it allowed one to explore, and the Victorian worship of Exercise, which is what it took to do it.

A wheelmen's outing for Victorian Lovers could explore one of the nearby scenic routes to raise public awareness of its beauty and encourage the establishment of public bike paths. The Victorian angle would enhance media coverage. Or the occasion might be tied into a bicycle race. Better yet, it might take the form of a bicycle tour of Victorian homes with the ladies dressed like Gibson Girls.

"Penny farthing" bicycles like those in the poster (left) were visually outstanding but impractical; the slightest rise in the road could become a "heartbreak hill." More sensible was the bicycle formidably piloted by a Gibson Girl (far right).

CARBING UP

Since modern wheelmen load up with carbohydrates before an outing, called "carbing up," you have the opportunity for a verandah breakfast focused on a Victorian breakfast breads, pancakes, waffles, fresh summer fruits, and a variety of cereals, especially oatmeal.

Queen Victoria, during an early visit to Scotland, asked why the wee laddies and lassies looked so healthy. "They are fed oatmeal porridge every morning, ma'am," was the reply. She fed it to her own children; others in England and America followed suit.

If your wheelmen are going to wallow in carbohydrates, fill their plates with wonderful breads and muffins warm from the oven.

Victorian wheelmen were no different from today's when it came to counting calories; they let the meter RUN.

Oatmeal doesn't have to be boring. Adding raisins, currants, figs, dates, or dried apricots after it has boiled gives it color accents, changes in texture and natural sweetening. Extra color and sweetening can be added with trendy "raw" or unrefined sugars like date sugar or Demerara. Other accents are buckwheat honey, molasses or maple syrup. Scots are said to abhor sugars of any kind, requiring only a dash of salt. It is also said they never mix milk into it. Bowls of thick cream are provided for coating spoonfuls of oatmeal before they are popped into mouths.

Serving hot cereals for either a plain or fancy breakfast is the equivalent of the soup course in a dinner menu. Special cereal bowls are not required; serve it in soup plates. "If one has nothing for [breakfast but cereal, eggs, and muffins], put them on the table in style; serve them in three courses, and one will imagine it a much better [breakfast] than if carelessly served," said Mrs. Henderson.

Porridge

Jessup Whitehead's 1893 *Steward's Handbook* lists twenty-eight kinds of porridge for breakfast, pointing out that it is the "proper name of 'mush,' which is but a provincialism. Made of oatmeal, cornmeal, graham meal, fine hominy or grits, ground rice, farina, cracked wheat, rolled oats, etc." An oddity is "English Furmety ...whole wheat porridge with milk and currants added."

There are dozens of cooked cereals that can be enhanced with nuts, fruits, and sugars.

LAWN GAMES LUNCHEON

*Two agitated young ladies interrupt the family gardener's
digging in the side lawn. One shouts, "Going to make a
flower-bed here Smithers! Why, it'll quite spoil our Croquet
Ground!" Smithers wryly replies, "Well, that's yer Pa's orders,
Miss. He'll hev' it laid out for 'Orticultur', not for 'Usbandry!"*

Harper's Weekly, October 5, 1867

Lost your ball? Someone you thought was your friend just whacked it with apparent malice? Mallets have been raised in anger? Clearly, it's time to break for love with a luncheon on the grass.

This illustration from Harper's Weekly *June 29, 1867, depicts the Victorian mating season played out around a derivative of croquet called* martelle. *Notice the seated gentleman on the left with tensely twined legs and cane bent nearly to the breaking point. Obviously, the lady of his ardor has used the Victorian "language of the fan" to good effect.*

SUMMER WAS THE VICTORIAN MATING SEASON. Families that couldn't go abroad followed the horses from The Derby in May to Saratoga in August. Mating, for families that had summer places, gave an extra dimension to courting lawn games.

CROQUET AND ITS DERIVATIVES

After the Civil War, various kinds of croquet became a national craze. Billiards, a royal French game played by both men and women well into the nineteenth century, was the ancestor of croquet along with a version of what would now be called "miniature golf." A new kind of croquet called Martelle appeared in New York in 1867. According to *Harper's Weekly*, "'The Queen of the Lawn' combines some of the attractive features of billiards, ten-pins, and Croquet." Instead of whacking a ball through a hoop, pins are knocked down; rubber-edged "reflectors" are used for billiard-like caroms (from the French for "cannon"); golf-cup "wells" are hazards which lead to penalty points.

Martelle

Martelle is a Victorian lawn game that might be revived and added to the standard croquet set. All that would be necessary are the "brightly painted" single circular and six elliptical rubber-edged wooden reflectors decorated in a Victorian fashion, six plastic "wells," a well cutter, and "gay guidons" or boundary flags. What recommended it then may recommend it now: "It is in many respects an improvement on Croquet, which is sometimes tedious and monotonous, Martelle being more varied in its play than the former game, more ingenious in its combinations, and more rapid in its movements. The players are kept constantly on the alert, which is not the case with Croquet, and an interest is excited which soon absorbs and fascinates the players." But the chief attraction of Martelle and croquet was "the little coquetries and gay flirtations which summer pastimes may innocently include."

Victorians converted a barn or stable into a bowling alley (above). By miniaturizing bowling, croquet, and martelle, they were able to convert parlor tabletops into gaming surfaces for family fun (left).

Badminton and Bowling

Another form of courting was badminton. This could take place today without the excessive competitiveness characteristic of lawn tennis, which some of the company might take too seriously.

Another summer sport for mixed company is bowling. Few, if any, Victorian bowling alleys survive, but an illustration from a *Harper's Weekly* for 1869 is suggestive of how it might be possible to create one in a basement, garage, or barn. Or a shuffleboard court might be converted to ten-pins.

LUNCHEON

As lawn games in one form or another can be played during the course of an afternoon, the luncheon should be light and remain available throughout the play. If anything Victorian is to be featured in the food beyond some of the classic summer picnic or luncheon fare, let it be Victorian temperance drinks—not so much for the sake of temperance, but the exploration of tasty natural beverages like fruit vinegars, fruit shrubs, lemonades, teas, switchel, ginger beer, dulcets, cups, etc. There are a large number of which most are far more refreshing and healthy on a hot summer day than any alcoholic drink. An old recipe for a fruit shrub is: One Sour (Lemon); Two Sweet (Sugar); Three Strong (Spirits); Four Weak (Water).

© R. Rubiera/FPG International

© William Seitz

Cold, homemade lemonade served in simple glasses; lattice-topped fruit pies; thick slices of fresh bread—this is a field of honor for a summer day of Victorian lawn games.

Make Your Own Hammock

A pretty and very comfortable hammock can be made of awning-cloth. Two pieces, six feet long and a little over a yard wide, are cut for the bottom of the hammock; and two strips, five inches wide, to go along the sides. These are scalloped and bound with worsted braid, and the strips basted in place between the two large pieces. The side seams are sewed up on the wrong side. After being turned right side out, the two ends are bound with braid. Eight curtain rings are sewed on each end, and to each ring is fastened a heavy hammock cord. These cords are all joined to a large iron ring. To hang the hammock, a light rope is passed through the rings and around two trees or posts.

A hammock should be hung where there is good afternoon shade. If intended in part for children's use, hang it low enough that small children can get into it by the aid of a box or low stool, and over soft ground, so that the numerous tumbles that are probable will be harmless. If no other place is available, it may be hung between the pillars of a shady veranda, a place well enough for the older people who use it, but undesirable for children, on account of the lack of a soft turf, as well as for the noise which accompanies its use by the youngsters. When children are only to use the hammock, the manner of hanging it is not important, but if provided for the use of grown persons, it should then be so suspended that the head will always be considerably

© William Seitz

higher than the foot, and much of the comfort of the one who uses this depends upon a proper observance of this fact. The hook which supports the head end, is six and one-fourth feet from the floor, and that for the foot end is three and three-fourths feet, and these proportions should be observed wherever it may be hung, to secure the most desirable curve for the ease of the occupant. Another point to be observed; the head end is fastened to the hook by a rope less than a foot long—just enough to properly attach it, while at the foot is a rope four and a half feet long. This gives the greatest

freedom for swinging the lower part of the body, while the head moves but little. This is a point which cannot be observed in a hammock for children, who think more of it as a swing than as a place for comfortable repose. When trees serves as supports, ample provisions should be made to prevent injury to the bark, by means of stout canvas or heavy bagging between the ropes to which it is suspended and the bark. If the hanging be so arranged that the hammock can be taken in during long storms, it will last much longer.

Household Conveniences, 1884

Victorians converted a functional South American Indian net sleeping sling into an enduring symbol of leisure and laziness. By 1879, St. Nicholas *magazine was instructing children how to weave a hammock. "In the Hammock" (above) is from* At Home Again, *part of a series of important British Aesthetic Movement children's books published by Marcus Ward in the 1880s. Such images of aesthetic languor had a big impact on Late Victorian adults as well as children.*

JULY FOURTH NEIGHBORHOOD PICNIC AND PARADE

It is not necessary for many people to be interested at first in the celebration, to make the same a success. The resolve by one person to have a grand celebration, who will call a public meeting, associate with two others as an executive committee, and follow by the appointment of the necessary committees, publishing the whole to the world, and going ahead, will generally make a very successful celebration.

"Celebrations and Festivals" in
Hill's Manual of Social & Business Forms, 1883

Though the technology of fireworks has changed considerably since the nineteenth century, the enthusiasm with which adults and children alike watch them was as bright then as it is today.

THE FOURTH IS ONE OF THREE AMERICAN holidays for which the menus have been established by Victorian tradition. The other two are Thanksgiving and Christmas. That's why it isn't necessary to tell you what to eat on The Fourth— you already know.

The hot dog was not an American invention, being developed out of German sausages and sometimes honoring the old association with names like "frankfurter" or "wiener," or their nicknames, "frank" and "weenie." But, according to *Sodom by the Sea: An Affectionate History of Coney Island* by Pilat and Ranson (1941), the name "hot dog" was invented circa 1906 by Tad Dorgan, a New York newspaper cartoonist, who also coined the immortal phrase, "Yes, we have no bananas."

If it rains on your July Fourth parade and you have to take the festivities indoors, don't despair. Bring the flags and bunting into the dining room, and the spirit of '76 will follow.

A VICTORIAN PARADE

Today, when most Americans abandon their homes and hit the road for distant parks and beaches, it might make sense to reconsider The Fourth in a Victorian context and celebrate closer to home. In fact, so many Americans leave town on this holiday that home towns are often quite tranquil. But the greatest benefit of staying close to home is the opportunity for community redevelopment.

A parade on The Fourth is doggedly carried on in most American communities, but it is a ghost of its Victorian self when everybody participated. It only takes one look at an old picture of a Victorian parade on The Fourth to realize what has been lost. The art of decorating with flags and bunting is gone. Not only commercial districts got decorated, but also private homes. On the porch posts and columns of many Victorian homes one can still locate the old flag standards for as many as six or eight small flags.

Celebrate a Victorian Fourth, by supporting the community parade, decorating for it, and inviting your family and neighborhood friends for a picnic on the verandah, on the lawn, in the garden, or in a park.

A VICTORIAN PICNIC

The Fourth was a traditional Victorian time for grass-roots politicking, hence the old political and fraternal "chowder and marching" societies. Contrary to common sense, hot food does not make one hotter than cold food, so a chowder

or clambake is in order for this mid-summer celebration. In addition to the hot doggery of the American Fourth, one might explore other forms of sausage. In addition to traditional lemonade, one might explore old-fashioned root beer or birch beer, and try to make some at home, if possible. During the nineteenth and twentieth centuries, class and ethnic distinctions have been associated with the drinking of

© Steven Mark Needham/Envision

beer and ale. This is the time to put them aside and support the growing number of small-production, old-fashioned beer and ale breweries. You will discover serious beer and ale societies that arrange tastings in the mode of wine tastings.

Along with the beer and ale, have a game of horseshoes. It's easy to make a horseshoe "pitch" and the shoes are readily available in any sports store. The pins are two iron pipes. It's great fun and especially appropriate for a Victorian Fourth.

The Fourth is the time for fresh summer fruits of any kind, especially in homemade ice cream. Hand-cranked or motor-driven freezers are available, as well as recipe books. For those who don't want to consume quite so much butterfat but still want fresh fruit flavors, make sherbets.

Soup is not out of the question for a summer picnic, along with the other common picnic victuals. A memorable climax to the event would be the hand-cranking and eating of homemade ice creams. You might use a motor-driven ice cream maker, but that would deny everyone the pleasure of making a physical investment in dessert. Afterwards, a few calories could be worked off with a game or two of horseshoes.

HENLEY ROYAL REGATTA BUFFET OR PICNIC

Thomas Eakins, "Max Schmitt in a Single Scull," The Metropolitan Museum of Art, Purchase, Alfred N. Punnett Endowment Fund and George D. Pratt Gift, 1934

The quiet beauty of shells moving across the water has been appreciated by spectators since before the Henley Royal Regatta was established in 1839.

Henley-on-Thames is the site of the annual race that is perhaps the most quintessential British spectacle, enjoyed almost continuously since its establishment in 1839. Dozens of nations participate in the event. Yet, as Lady Clementine Churchill once told Winston, it is a "lovely pageant of English life." The race was born when the town fathers noted that races were being held on the river at Henley, a perfect natural course. They decided that "from the lively interest which has been manifested at the various boat races," an annual regatta "under judicious and respectable management" would amuse and gratify the neighborhood "from its peculiar attractions." The peculiar qualities of Henley are still intact, not the least of which are the "judicious" Stewards. These zealous protectors, appointed for life, make certain that all conduct is proper for the event. The slightest offense is greeted with a curt, "Not at Henley, please." And that is that.

Benjamin Ivry, *Regatta,* 1988

Ladies bedecked in their summer best; hats of every style imaginable; cold lobster and strawberry tea; parasols and huge umbrellas— all these things help create the special atmosphere of the Henley Royal Regatta.

ROWING HAS BEEN AN ELEGANT PART OF the British tradition since Handel's famous "Water Music" was played on the royal barge to amuse the King and his Court while they were rowed up the Thames River to Hampton Court.

After the Civil War, American colleges as well as private clubs organized their own regattas. The most famous collection of Late Victorian clubs and boathouses are those that line Boathouse Row on the Schuylkill River in Philadelphia, formally organized in 1875 as The Schuylkill Navy.

ELEGANT DINING ON THE RIVER

Regattas always take place on beautiful rivers and lakes, so the natural setting should enhance a delightful summer afternoon eating alfresco. Henley is the excuse for a thoroughly British summer buffet or picnic taken to the site in great hampers and served up in as elegant a manner as possible. The key is chilled champagne and fresh strawber-

© Patrick Walmsley/Envision

North Wind Picture Archives

Spread a blanket under a tree on a rise up from the river, and you are sure to have a good view of the races below.

the card easel-fashion. *The napery was folded* à la bateaux, *and the gunwales formed of violets, snowdrops, and primroses, intertwined with light foliage and mounted on wire, so that they were readily removed by the guests and kept in form without the untidy litter often caused by the insertion of loose sprays in the serviettes. In the center of the table was an epergne filled with fruit and flowers. In the middle of the large glass dish, on the top, was an Undine boat, filled with flowers, and an exquisite wax model of Undine, the water spirit, in their midst. The boat was surrounded by fruits and flowers of the most expensive class, inter-mixed with young palm-leaves and natural grasses. At the foot, beside the claws (representing the four lions* couchant), *were groups of little sailor dolls, representing the crews and their friends, no doubt, some with small polished oars, others with flags, and a couple with flagons in their hands. The* tout ensemble *was very pretty.*

ries, served with thick cream or dipped in powdered sugar. Common Victorian picnic or buffet fare in the British tradition is cold meat pies like the famous "Cornish Pasty" of miners, or the pastry-encased "Scotch Eggs." More elegant would be a paté or special cold chicken dish. Sliced tongue would supply a savory meat. But the most elegant of all would be a chilled whole poached salmon.

From Whitehead's *Steward's Handbook* of 1893, here is "A Boating Club's Fantasy," which should inspire you with decorative ideas for the event:

The table was decorated with glass ware in the shape of small boats mounted on plateaux of looking-glass, surrounded by sage-green plush borders, fringed by silk blond lace of a lighter shade. The boats rested on four glass oars, crossed at either side, and forming a stand. Light trailing foiliage [hung] from the boats, and trailed on the glass plateaux. Spring flowers from the sunny South filled the boats and nestled amidst ferns and mosses arranged round the gunwales. At the prows of the larger-sized bateaux *were little flags and ensigns. Small glass boats were laid at each cover, filled with dark-blue violets and French or Italian grown forget-me-nots in alternate boats. The violets for the gentlemen, the light-blue flowers for the fair visitors. The* menus *were printed on cards representing a yacht's sail, silver-edged and supported at the back by an oar, which fixed*

This Harper's Weekly *illustration from June 26, 1875 shows Columbia University's architect-designed boat-house by John C. Babcock. Literally a Boat House, it floated in the Harlem River and cost $10,000.*

VICTORIAN WEDDING BREAKFAST

© Robert Perron

Should a breakfast or supper follow the ceremony, the bride will not change her dress until she assumes her traveling apparel. At the wedding breakfast or supper the bride sits by the side of her husband, in the center of the table, at the side; her father and mother occupy the foot and head of the table, and do the honors of the occasion, as at the dinner-party.

"Celebrations and Festivals," in
Hill's Manual of Social & Business Forms, 1883

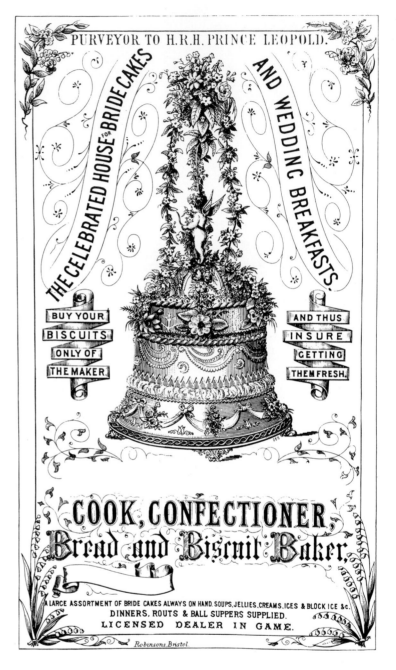

WEDDING BREAKFAST WAS A VICTORIAN RITE. Actually, according to Whitehead's 1893 *Steward's Handbook*, it "is really an elaborate luncheon and not the breakfast ordinarily understood."

If you don't have a wedding in your near future, you might do the same kind of entertainment for an anniversary or a graduation. If you serve the food outdoors under a tent, consider the Victorian tent described on page 101.

© Matthew Klein

An all-white place setting is an appropriate field for the food of a wedding breakfast, but the flowers and the cake are what will be remembered by your guests, hence the sizable investment made in them.

A wedding breakfast in the Victorian grand manner was a multi-course meal with a light, but elegant soup served in a beautiful tureen, followed by roast fowls.

THREE WEDDING MENUS

From Whitehead's *Steward's Handbook*, here are some Wedding Breakfast menus. The first is the cheapest at about two dollars per head, 1893 money.

Consommé à la Victoria
Aspic of Prawns and Lobster Salad
Roast Fowls and Cumberland Ham
Roast Lamb and Pressed Beef
Swiss Cake and Fruit Jellies
Strawberry Cream and Lemon Water Ices
Dessert and Bonbons

The Consommé à la Victoria is a printaniere or "clear soup with small-cut spring vegetables, string beans, peas, asparagus points with chicken-quenelles reddened with lobster coral." The Cumberland Ham is probably country ham. The Swiss Cake is probably a Swiss Roll—a rolled sponge cake with filling. The Pressed Beef is cold, pickled beef.

For this wedding, a long table was decorated with a border of flowers about a foot wide just inside the table settings. In this border at each setting rose "rustic branches" supporting individual menus printed silver on a white ground. The wedding cake was the centerpiece. "The table napkins were folded like tents, the bridegroom being an officer in the army."

The next wedding was slightly more expensive at two-and-a-half dollars per head.

Strawberry cream was featured in the sweet finale of a Late Victorian wedding breakfast.

MENU

Consommé à la Nelson
Mayonnaise of Salmon and Lobster Patties
Lamb Cutlets and Green Peas
Capons Béchamel à la Belle Vue
Galantine of Veal and Game Pies
Italian Salad
Wine Jellies and Velvet Cream
Charlotte à la Parisienne
Chocolate and Strawberry Ices
Dessert and Bonbons

The Consommé à la Nelson is a clear fish soup with rice. The Galantine of Veal is a cold sausage of veal cased in its own jelly.

This bridegroom was a naval officer, so the table was decorated "with little satin flags, suggestive of a ship on some great holiday. From the cake (forming the center of highest mast) [hung] silk ropes to each place setting, on which were threaded the tiny flags. These were terminated by a china figure of a sailor boy holding the menu to each guest. The menu was very pale blue, printed in a deeper shade. The table-napkins folded like boats, and the most beautiful seaweeds were mixed with the flowers."

Frost your favorite cake with butter cream frosting and decorate with white chocolate rosettes—your wedding guests will rave.

Finally, here is a wedding menu that was twice as expensive at five dollars per head. Note that the number of French names rises in proportion to the price.

Potage aux Huîtres and Consommé à la Royale
Salade d'Homard Monté
Pâté de Fois Gras à la Gelée
Suprême de Volaille aux Truffes
Roulades braisé à la Royale
Mayonnaise de Saumon à la Montpellier
Petits Poulets aux Campignons and Quails
Gateaux à la Lorne and Meringues au Café Mocha
Gelées aux Ponche et d'Or
Fanchonettes à la Crême
Chocolate Cream and Cherry Water Ices
Dessert and Bonbons

Then as now, cutting the cake was the climax of the reception.

Potage aux Huîtres is oyster soup. Consommé à la Royale is bits of precisely cut chicken, mushrooms, and truffles sandwiched between a molded egg and cream mixture flavored with nutmeg and served with chicken consommé. The Salade d'Homard is lobster salad. Pâté de Fois Gras à la Gelée is made from the fat liver of a goose and served in a gelatin case. Suprême de Volaille is chicken breasts enhanced with truffles.

The setting for each guest at this wedding was marked by a floral arch "under which stood a little alabaster figure, holding the menu. Arches were also formed over the principal dishes, these being surmounted by tiny white and red satin flags, bearing the united monograms of the bride and groom."

Another possible setting was a large square table for twenty-eight, formed from four smaller square tables. A large cake was the centerpiece of "a sloping bank made all round to come about eighteen inches on to the table. From this raised bank twenty-eight festoons of flowers depended, each terminating opposite a guest, and finished by a little cupid holding the menu, which was white satin bordered with a row of small pearls."

© Robert Kaufman

"In all cases the entire service was of white china. The waiters wore white gloves during the breakfast. Crimson cloth was laid on the front steps and down to the carriages."

In these descriptions, there is little in the menus to suggest anything appropriate to the season or the occasion. Note that the bridegroom's career determined special decorations, not the bride's. It appears that the flowers were more important than the food, as long as there was plenty to eat and drink. This suggests that June and summer weddings were popular for the cheap supply of fresh flowers. Little has changed, although wedding flowers now come from commercial sources no longer dependent on season.

If a napkin fold or a table decoration or a food can be connected to one or both of the persons being married, there is ample Victorian precedent.

WEDDING CAKES A SPECIALITY.

© Robert Kaufman

How To Make A Tent

"A Home-Made Tent" is a practical setting for your Victorian garden or lawn parties, which could easily be made today out of white plastic PVC plumbing pipe and modern awning cloth and will cost a tenth or less than what is charged for today's neo-Victorian wooden gazebos.

The top is in one piece, and to it are sewed the side pieces and those for the ends, cut in scallops around the lower edge and bound with woolen braid, of a color to correspond with that of the stripe in the cloth. The pieces must all be sewed together very firmly, and the seams bound on the wrong side. Cords are attached to each corner of the cover, by which it is tied to the frame. If the tent is to stand in a very exposed situation, where there is an entire absence of shade, an extra curtain will be desirable. This should be supplied with rings, and hung on the side needing the protection from the sun. Two frames may be put up; one on that part of the lawn which is the most pleasant in the morning, and the other in a favorite after-dinner gathering place. If the frames are of the same size, one cover will do for both. In this way, two tents can be made but with little more trouble and expense than one.

Household Conveniences, 1884

In love, hearts are trump; but at weddings, flowers ace the food. Elaborately ornamented Victorian houses were often called "wedding cake" houses. Examples like this (far left) are the reason why.

VICTORIAN SHORE DINNER

The sun is setting, sending fingers of color onto low-lying clouds. The senses are exposed; you can hear the waves, feel the mist in the evening air, and smell the change in the tide.

Naomi Black, *Seashore Entertaining*, 1987

SHORE VERSUS MOUNTAINS WAS A DECISION that wealthy Victorians never had to make; they visited both! The time and expense of getting to the mountains was what limited the choice to the shore for other Victorians, shores being closer to major cities than mountains and easily reached by railroads and boats for day trips and short visits.

Beaches everywhere have a unique and compelling beauty that makes any visit to them a special event.

National Museum of American Art, Smithsonian Institution

SHORE RESORTS

The earliest shore resorts were developed between New York and Philadelphia along the New Jersey coast with Cape May at the southern tip being the first. Developed by Philadelphia families as early as 1795, Cape May is still one of the most desirable seaside resorts and revels in its extraordinary collection of seaside cottages, villas, and bed and breakfast inns, many of which are delightfully colored.

At the other end of New Jersey, the fashionable resort was Long Branch immortalized by Winslow Homer's paintings and illustrations for *Harper's Weekly*. It was a favorite

From Bar Harbor, Maine to the Florida Keys, the Orcas Islands in Washington State to San Diego, California, Dover to the Isle of Man in Great Britain, there are a myriad of wonderful shore resorts to explore and experience.

Hand coloring by Melissa Dehncke

summer place for presidents like General Grant, even spawning a "Long Branch" cottage style that was emulated on Long Island and elsewhere.

As with the lawn games, a visit to the shore gave young people a chance to get together in a much less formal atmosphere than the home. The chief source of jokes was Victorians taking their formal, domestic manners and clothing to the beach. It might be fun to dress up Victorian style at the beach as long as one never went into the water. The gowns and pajamas make it difficult for even good swimmers to escape the grip of the undertow.

Fashion trod the sands when Victorians went to the shore. In these days of lobster scarcity, we can only envy the fellow who has grabbed one at the shoreline.

Autumn

TALLY-HO OR HUNT BREAKFAST

Gone are the days when riders had a separate suit of clothes for their jaunts and ladies rode side saddle. Someone in your crowd may have a pair of jodphurs, and others may be able to piece together an outfit that closely resembles a habit—that will just add to the fun.

*He shared cheerfully in all the amusements of his little set—rode,
played polo, hunted and drove his four-in-hand with the
best of them (you will see by the last allusion,
that we were still in the archaic 'nineties).*

Edith Wharton, *The Spark*, 1924

*Paraphernalia of the horsey crowd always includes a substantial
amount of leather and cups (left). Your invitations to a tally-ho event
could resemble the ticket pictured above.*

HORSE TRANSPORT WAS STILL ESSENTIAL for short distances in 1900, but by the 1880's Victorian railroads had made the old four-horse "tally-ho" or "four-in-hand" as obsolete as open fireplaces. The new-money society of the Late-Victorian period transformed both the fireplace and the tally-ho into venerable symbols of a golden age they called "The Olden Time." Edith Wharton, in *The Spark*, describes their lifestyle as a country house "full of portraits, of heavy mahogany furniture and the mingled smell of lavender bags and leather—leather boots, leather gloves, leather luggage, all the aromas that emanate from the cupboards and passages of a house inhabited by hard riders."

From the first flowers to the first snows, they rode to hounds and had Hunt Balls, Hunt Suppers, and Hunt Breakfasts. The high point of the season was the parade of the old tally-ho coaches. Today, this is preserved at some of the surviving hunts, point-to-point races, and horse shows.

If you don't have any of these events handy, you could organize a country walk and call it a "hunt." Like Derby Day in the Spring, you could decorate with horse paraphernalia. Here is the menu and decor for a British Hunt Breakfast. Obviously, this is the occasion for an extensive autumn menu filled with all the stereotypical British Breakfast items.

A breakfast table can be set more casually, with placemats instead of a lace tablecloth. Beautiful china, however, will make the first meal of the day just that much more special.

Broiled Kidneys and Pulled Fowl
Salmon Steaks and Stuffed Tomatoes
Sheeps Tongues and Potted Pigeons
Broiled Rump Steaks and Quenelles
Croquettes of Rice and Ham
Chickens in Béchamel
Potted Game and Pâté Mele
Cold Sirloin of Beef and Pressed Tongues
York Hams and Raised Pies (various)
Normandy Pippins and Stewed Prunes
Clotted Cream
Roast Snipes and Wood Cocks and Thrushes
Apple Marmelade and Apricot Jam
and Currant Jelly
Vanilla Milk and Cafe au Lait and
Tea Liqueurs

© R. Embery/FPG International

"Breakfast at Bonnebouche Hall" by George du Maurier, shows a hunt breakfast with its self-service from a side board, immense urn on the table, and the ubiquitous dog.

The tables on this occasion were dressed with white cloths and decorated à la jardinère. *The silver antique jardinières were filled with ferns and spring flowers, peeping out of mosses of various kinds. Large silver bowls and epergnes of the side-board and side tables were filled with exquisite arrangements of hyacinths, tulips, wood violets, snowdrops, etc., in mosaic patterns; whilst hanging baskets graced the windows, filled with the spiritulle cyclamen light foliage, interspersed with yellow and red flowers, that gave the grand old oak hall a splendid appearance. The display of antique plate would have delighted the heart of the most enthusiastic antiquary. The vanilla milk, which, by the way, was half cream, found great favor, and was served steaming hot in silver cups. Some added curacoa to it, others a petit verre de Cognac,* but the majority preferred the sweet beverage simply as prepared in the kitchen by my worthy old friend, the *chef.*

Jessup Whitehead, *Steward's Handbook*, 1893

SHUNPIKER'S PICNIC

The excitement of a shunpiker's picnic is the discovery of a beautiful country scene (above). Picnic baskets evoke romance with their simplicity and their promise of treasures and pleasures inside (right).

The Picnic season is at hand, and will stir up those who, "Sick of home and luxuries, Do want a new sensation." What visions of unbridged brooks to be crossed, etc. And then—to come to more material things—what a singular turn your appetite took for ham sandwiches and other picnic fare!

Harper's Weekly, June 5, 1858

SHUNPIKING IS AN OLD TERM FOR "GETTING OFF the beaten path." All that anyone will discover on today's turnpikes and interstate highways is the dull, commercialized sameness of America. To make contact with local differences one has to shun the pike. This might be turned into a pleasant celebration by "shunpiking" your horseless carriage to a picnic in the country. Here is an "Automobile Hamper" filled with food from a 1910 menu supplied by a Rochester, New York processor of canned foods.

Menu

Mock Turtle Soup
Olives   Celery
Sandwiches à la Motor
Minced Chicken
Red Currant Jelly
Cold Sliced Ham & Turkey
Brandy Peaches
Basket Salad
Speed-a-Way Sponge Cake
Cheese
Cherry Jam
Raspberry Shrub

© Daniel Needham/Envision

MENU

AUTOMOBILE HAMPER

Blue Label Mock Turtle Soup
Olives   Celery
★Sandwiches à la Motor
Minced Chicken
Red Currant Jelly
Cold Sliced Ham
Cold Roast Turkey
Brandy Peaches
★Basket Salad
★Speed-a-Way-Sponge Cake
(Special)
Cheese   Cherry Jam
Raspberry Shrub

AUTOMOBILE HAMPER

BASKET SALAD.

ILL. 2.—Remove seeds of ½ dozen Green Peppers, cut in form of baskets, fill with chopped CURTICE Wax Beans, cubes of CURTICE Red Beets and pimentos with French dressing.

SPEED-A-WAY SPONGE CAKE.

ILL. 1.—3 eggs; 1 cup sugar; 4 tablespoons milk; 1 cup flour; teaspoon baking powder, lemon flavor. Bake in square tin—cut in squares. Remove small portions from center of each square, fill with CURTICE Cherry Jam. Decorate with icing and CURTICE preserved Cherries.

SANDWICHES A LA MOTOR.

ILL. 3—Shape very thin slices of sandwichbread with cake cutter. Remove portions of upper layer to form wheels. Spread with CURTICE Devilled or Potted Ham.

Before the automobile became a necessity, it was a toy used by rich city folks for the ride in the country. Even then, modern technology rode in the "automobile hamper" as well as under the hood; most of this 1910 menu above was poured out of bottles filled by Curtice-Burns, a Rochester, New York food processor.

The baskets of the salad were made from bell peppers and filled with wax beans, red beets, pimientos, and French dressing. Sandwiches à la Motor are circle sandwiches with the top layer cut out to form spokes. Speed-a-Way Sponge Cake is sponge cake filled with cherry jam, with tops iced and decorated with preserved cherries.

If you prefer a spirit of adventure, pack your hampers with only the necessities and try to "live off the land" as much as possible. Foraging in the autumnal countryside will be the chief delight of the event—hunting out the roadside stands, local markets, and farmers for homemade bread, root beer, pickles, relishes, jams, vegetables, meats, pies, and cakes.

© John Domiris/Wheeler Pictures

© Joe Viesti/Viesti Associates, Inc.

COSTUME DRESS AND A RURAL SETTING

Since there is little difference in the minds of most between the Victorian and Edwardian periods (i.e. the nineteenth and early twentieth centuries), one could dress up with old goggles and dusters and make believe you were back in the horseless carriage days. If you wanted to give it a name you could call it an "Excuse My Dust Picnic," which offers the ancillary pleasures of shunpiking and exploring some of the less travelled byways of your region.

Even a major purchase from a farmer's roadside stand will not buy you the privilege of using the farmer's field for a picnic site without permission. Dress plainly so the farmer can see you instead of your city fashions. When asking permission, make assurances that you are there to celebrate the countryside and will leave the site neat and tidy. Say this without anticipation of approval. The farm family that says "yes" might remain your country friends long after you have left. If you don't want to leave this to chance, writing in advance to the county chamber of commerce might provide a list of public picnic areas but that would defeat the adventurous purpose of "The Shunpiker's Picnic."

GUY FAWKES DAY SUPPER

Oh!—fruit loved of boyhood!—the old days recalling,
When wood-grapes were purpling and brown nuts were falling!
When wild, ugly faces we carved in its skin,
Glaring out through the dark with a candle within!

John Greenleaf Whittier, "The Pumpkin Effigy,"
from *Harper's Weekly*, November 23, 1867

© Jerry Howard/Positive Images

American jack-o'-lanterns of modern halloween fame were appropriated from the "pumpkin effigies" of Guy Fawkes Day in Britain. This is from Harper's Weekly, *November 23, 1867.*

GUY FAWKES DAY IS NAMED FOR A BRITISH folk hero and his failed Gunpowder Plot of 1605 to blow up the Old Houses of Parliament which later burned shortly before Queen Victoria's Coronation and were rebuilt in their present Gothic Revival form. Guy Fawkes Day was celebrated in Victorian England by fireworks, bonfires, and children begging "a penny for the Guy," with his effigy made from a carved turnip for the head and a long stick for the body clothed with an old coat. Guy Fawkes Day was celebrated in Victorian North America, especially by New Englanders. It was eventually replaced by modern Halloween, which appropriated its festivities, especially the "pumpkin effigy" better known as the jack-o'-lantern.

© B. March/FPG International

Since Guy Fawkes Day has all the good parts of Halloween—the bonfire, the fireworks, the jack-o'-lantern, and the Autumn food—it's a Victorian entertainment that can be revived to avoid all the bad parts of Halloween. Because it's celebrated November 5, pumpkins for Guy Fawkes effigies can be had free or bought at bargain prices. If you can find one that is large and handsome without being huge, you can use it as the functional centerpiece of your Guy Fawkes Supper for a hearty pumpkin soup. Serve it with plenty of hot corn bread, a salad, and freshly-made sweet cider for a satisfying Autumnal feast. For dessert, instead of pumpkin pie (which should be reserved for Thanksgiving), make a rich nut cake from walnuts or hickory nuts.

That nip in the air, those glorious colors, the piles of Nature's bounty—autumn is a delightful season best celebrated with food featuring fruits, nuts, and vegetables. Fruit pies, a pumpkin soup, and a nut cake would be a blessing to any festive meal.

THANKSGIVING DINNER

What moistens the lip, and what brightens the eye?
What calls back the past, like the rich pumpkin pie?

John Greenleaf Whittier, "The Pumpkin Effigy,"
from *Harper's Weekly*, November 23, 1867

© Brian Leatart

For most Americans, Thanksgiving Day is "turkey day." It's more than an economical main course for large numbers of guests; its a symbolic rite.

THANKSGIVING IS AN ANCIENT CELEBRATION, going back many centuries before the famous feast of 1621 at Plimoth Plantation in New England. It is the medieval Harvest Festival or "Harvest Home" of Pilgrim rural England transferred to the New World. Recent research reveals that the first Pilgrim Thanksgiving took place in October, which is a more logical time for a Harvest Festival than the last Thursday in November. Canadian Thanksgiving takes place October 10, closer to the original.

Thanksgiving has been held in November in the United States for the last two hundred years, since George Washington transformed Harvest Home in 1789 into a celebration of the newly adopted Constitution. Lincoln made it a national holiday in 1863. Many credit this to Sarah Josepha Hale, a New Englander who promoted the poetry of national thanksgiving as editor of *Godey's*, the most popular Victorian magazine for ladies. Lincoln's reasoning, like that of Washington nearly seventy-five years earlier, had more political symbolism than poetic sensibility. Lincoln made Thanksgiving a national holiday at the same time he

THANKSGIVING

May your joys with the sunshine of life sweeter grow And each harvest season Thanksgiving bestow

It's difficult to separate fact from folklore, but the first American Thanksgiving was held in October and took the form of the medieval European harvest festivals.

was building the great dome of the Capitol; both were bold gestures of national unity. That's why all state Capitols built after the Civil War until the 1930s have a great dome modelled after the one in Washington; and why Thanksgiving remains an American national holiday in November.

If the commercialized poetry and patriotism of the Pilgrim Myth and The Flag sticks in your craw during Thanksgiving, celebrate it as the more ancient Harvest Home. Enjoy the bounties of Autumn Harvest and be grateful to live in a place where your family and friends can enjoy it.

A MEAL OF THE HARVEST

Courtesy New York Public Library

There isn't anything remarkably Victorian about Thanksgiving apart from the history of its American symbolism. Likewise the menu, which hasn't changed much during the many centuries that Autumn Harvest has been celebrated. The best Thanksgiving Dinner, quite simply, uses the finest local or home produce prepared in a superior manner. A healthy step in that direction has been taken during the last decade. Sales have risen significantly before Thanksgiving for fresh, undoctored turkeys, fresh pumpkin pies, and fresh cranberries.

© Brian Leatart

The bird can be beautiful, the vegetables can be delicious, the relishes can be sensational, but the ultimate success of Thanksgiving Dinner depends on dessert. In Hollywood terms, your meal is only as good as its last course, hence the traditional emphasis in American cooking on baked goods.

In Victorian times, the children were seated at a separate table, as in this Thanksgiving illustration from Harper's Weekly, *1858.*

The easiest way to Victorianize a Thanksgiving Dinner is to divide the meal into courses by starting with soup. If you want to add elegance to your menu with oysters, this is the place to do it. For something more substantial than oyster bisque, you might serve that favorite Victorian opener, scalloped oysters. Serving oysters either way would be safer than the Victorian and earlier method of using them in the stuffing. Using them in an equally traditional sauce would sacrifice them to enhancing the turkey, which should be good enough on its own merits.

A good soup course has two practical advantages. It gets consumed while the turkey is cooling to facilitate carving. And it prepares the way for the higher pleasures of the table by sharpening the appetite, while it dulls mere hunger.

Bountiful baskets of fruit make decorative centerpieces and provide an alternative to traditional Thanksgiving desserts.

Traditional Turkey

Thanksgiving, unlike other Victorian entertainments, allows only one choice for the main course—turkey, a native once promoted by Franklin as the symbolic national bird instead of the eagle with its Ancient Roman associations. You can alter the stuffing and the trimmings, but Thanksgiving without turkey isn't quite the same. That's why Turkey Day is the only holiday that can be identified by a food.

© Arthur Zippel/FPG International

© Guy Powers/Envision

Turkey with all the fixings is a meal that most people anticipate all year long (above). Succotash and pumpkin pie honor the gifts of native Americans to the Pilgrims and the world (right).

Succotash

The vegetable dishes are almost as traditional as the turkey. One that too often gets left out is succotash, which combines corn and beans—two gifts of the Americas via the Indians to the Pilgrims and the world. The best source for new ways to prepare these and other autumn vegetables is Marian Morash's *Victory Garden Cookbook*.

© Judd Pilossof

Pumpkin Pie

Thanksgiving pumpkin pie is the pie that inexperienced bakers will most often attempt because it is the easiest. Although great value is placed today on "making it from scratch," one may be excused from preparing the raw pumpkin. It's messy if you could find the right variety of pumpkin—not, incidentally, the pumpkin used for jack-o'-lanterns. Buy canned pumpkin and season it to your own taste by adding spices and flavoring. If making pie crust is intimidating, make the pumpkin filling as a custard served in ramekins. If your guests ask for an explanation, tell them that American Thanksgiving pumpkin pie developed out of English Harvest Home pudding and you are returning to its earlier form.

TEA DANCE

*Over the years the control of the dancing masters became greater,
and in 1879 a Society of Professors of Dancing was organized
for the purpose of advancing the art of dancing and for the
presentation of identical methods of instruction. As a result of
this, dancing for a time lost a good deal of
its originality and freshness.*

Sylvia Dannett and Frank Rachel,
Down Memory Lane, 1954

A TEA DANCE ALLOWS YOU TO FINESSE THE expense and bother of a Victorian ball while enjoying the pleasures of social dancing in the Victorian style. "Tea" was often used imprecisely by Victorians for an entertainment. For example, while sitting on a verandah on a summer Sunday afternoon one might be offered an impromptu invitation to "Sunday Tea," which turned out to be the family's Sunday Dinner or Sunday Supper. With a "tea" one can either serve only tea and cakes, making it into a dessert party, or serve more substantial food and alcoholic beverages to make it a supper.

If you decide to make your tea dance into a costume party, present the proposition to your guests as more vaguely than specifically Victorian. For most of the nineteenth century, women were sacramentalized in heavily upholstered dresses that made them look like extensions of the interior decor. It was not until the Aesthetic Movement of the 1870s, which focused on women as individual persons, that dresses became less fulsome and cumbersome. Today, your female guests are likely to be more comfortable in the trimmed blouses and lacy dresses that are sufficiently romantic to be perceived as "Victorian."

A tea dance might focus on one kind of Victorian dance like the waltz. Or it might be mixed with others like the less famous mazurka and schottische. Perhaps it would surprise many to learn that the polka was a nineteenth-century dance

© Brian Leatart

Victorian dessert services are some of the most handsome of artifacts, such as special ivory- or bone-handled silver cake servers and matched porcelain plates, platters, and pedestaled bowls. Sometimes champagne was served as well as tea.

that arrived in America in 1844. Its reputation was enhanced when Queen Victoria forbid it to be done in her sight.

You might schedule this entertainment in the late afternoon and terminate with a movie, play, or concert having a Victorian or Edwardian theme. This would allow you to have a dance party of limited duration at limited expense suitable for modern budgets and tolerance of such affairs.

You might set up a Palm Court with purchased or rented plants, a small string ensemble, hopefully provided by some of the guests for free. Some guests might dress as lounge lizards or gigolos or femmes fatales for extra fun.

Clearly this is the entertainment that might stretch "Victorian" to its maximum limit in the twentieth century. Such a dance could feature Victorian and Edwardian popular music, which exists in abundance on records and tapes. Or one might feature a movie with a Victorian setting on the VCR.

Courtesy Laura Ashley

Even if your house does not include an elegantly appointed formal parlor, you can play parlor games in any room.

There is a great library of popular, pompous, or posh Victorian piano music. New or old player pianos can bring much of it back to life; the fun will carry you back to the Victorian Era.

VICTORIAN PARLOR GAMES

In genteel Victorian parlance, games were either "lawn" or "parlor." Victorians would still recognize today's outdoor games, but they would be amazed by the electronic gadgetry of our indoor games. That's why today's Victorian entertainers will want to research low-tech Victorian parlor games and revive their personal favorites. Please remember that the ancestry of the Teutonic word "games" is rooted in the happy combination of amusement *and* companionship.

Here are some "round or parlour games" selected from a standard, Late Victorian, British guidebook also published in New York—*Cassell's Book of In-Door Amusements.*

Charades and Tableaux Vivants

The success of Tableaux, even more than Charades, depends very greatly upon dress and surroundings. Charades speak for themselves, but Tableaux are so soon over.—Cassell's Book of In-Door Amusements

© Michael Wilson/FPG International

Today's form of *Charades* uses monologue pantomimes to reveal a word or phrase. Victorian charades used short theatricals of audible dialogue to hide components of a word in separate "acts" and the complete word in the final "act." Cassell's provided an ABC list of over 100 words or phrases, including: artichoke, bookworm, catacomb, dovetail, earshot, footman, grandchild, homesick, intimate, joyful, kneedeep, loophole, moonstruck, nightmare, outside, padlock, quicksand, ringleader, sweetmeat, toadstool, uproar, vampire, wedlock, and youthful. A pile of "old clothes, shawls, and hats," along with other props, was provided to inspire the improvisation.

Tableaux Vivants were expensively staged and costumed arrangements of one person or many that either moved or were motionless. Favorite subjects were historic events, usually taken from Shakespeare, along with fairy tales, nursery rhymes, and Old Master paintings. An excellent description of a tableaux is in Edith Wharton's 1905 *The House of Mirth*. It opened with "a group of nymphs dancing across a flower-strewn sward in the rhythmic postures of Botticelli's Spring" and closed with a "a tribute, not to the brush-work of Reynolds's 'Mrs. Lloyd' but to the flesh and blood loveliness of Lily Bart."

A pile of elegant junk can be a treasure chest of inspiration for Victorian improvisations in such parlor games as charades *or* tableaux vivants.

Acting Proverbs and Acting Rhymes

Victorian moralizers to the middle class claimed the aristocracy and gentry didn't play games, but "gamed" or "gambled"; they had competitions instead of amusements. To a certain extent they were correct, for who enjoys being cleaned out or put down? Middle-class guides like Cassell's preferred games that "combine instruction with amusement" like *Acting Proverbs* or *Acting Rhymes*.

In either game, "each player may take a part or the company may divide themselves into actors and spectators." It would be helpful to provide a list of proverbs or words as well as some props to aid the uninspired. Acting out a proverb like "A rolling stone gathers no moss" is a kind of tableaux vivant. Pantomiming a sequence of rhymes to a word is akin to a modern charade.

Adjectives and Consequences

Adjectives is a jolly game of verbal nonsense something like today's Mad Libs. To begin, underline the adjectives in some suitable paragraphs taken from books or magazines. Then have your guests list six or more of their favorite adjectives. From this collection, substitute the underlined words as the paragraphs are read aloud. Or have one guest tell a little story, while another supplies adjectives from the collected lists.

Not all Victorian entertainments were organized. You may find it comforting to see in this Charles Dana Gibson illustration Victorians amusing themselves in the common fashion of sitting around talking. The joke here is "find the wife of the man who is telling the story." Gibson also showed Late Victorian gentry stuffed into overheated rooms, bored by pompous guests, and assaulted by incompetent musicians like "Mrs. Flatte Sharpe."

Another form of verbal nonsense is *Consequences*. Ask your guests to write on pieces of paper their responses to ten commands, each time folding over enough of the paper to cover what they have written, then passing their paper to the person on the right. The commands are: 1. One or more adjectives; 2. The name of a gentleman; 3. One or more adjectives; 4. A lady's name; 5. Where the man and lady met; 6. What he gave her; 7. What he said to her; 8. What she said to him; 9. The consequences; and 10. What the world said about it. After the last question, each guest reads aloud what is written on his or her paper.

Forfeits

Many young people think that the forfeits are greater fun than the games themselves, and that the best part of the evening begins when forfeit time arrives.

—Cassell's Book of In-Door
Amusements

Victorians often ended their evening of parlor games by playing a silly game that guaranteed that each would make at least one mistake for which they would be penalized with a forfeit. Finesse this and give everyone a forfeit to redeem. The hosts can assign these penalities in advance on cards in sealed envelopes, inventing a forfeit to suit the victim. Since the object of forfeits is to amuse the company with clever absurdities and not to make individuals appear inept, solutions to the forfeits should be provided on the backs of the cards. Some of Cassell's "good old-fashioned forfeits" are:

Bite an inch off the poker. Hold the poker an inch away from the mouth and take an imaginary bite.

Kiss the lady you love best without any one knowing it. Kiss all but the lady you love best.

Sit upon the fire. Write "The Fire" on a piece of paper and sit on it.

The German band. Imaginary musical instruments are "assigned to three or four of the company and upon these instruments they must perform as best they can."

Laugh in one corner of the room, sing in another, cry in another, and dance in another.

Kiss your own shadow. With a lighted candle, throw your shadow on the face of a friend, then kiss your friend's face.

Make your will. Make legacies to every person in the room, leaving such things, as your hair, eyebrows, wit, common sense, etc.

The cat's concert. Three or four people are assigned different songs that they must sing simultaneously.

No, the most popular Victorian after dinner amusement was not whisking off the table cloth, but balancing tricks, puzzles with match-sticks, and verbal games.

CASINO DESSERT

For card parties or small companies of thirty or forty persons, to meet some particular stranger, or for literary reunions, the trouble need not be great. People would entertain more if the trouble were less. Ices, cake, and chocolate are quite enough; or for chocolate might be substituted sherry or a bowl of punch.

Mary F. Henderson, *Practical Cooking and Dinner Giving*, 1876

© Brian Leatart

A card party, elevated by the term "Casino," which has not yet been totally bankrupted by Las Vegas and Atlantic City resorts, can accommodate a large company at modest expense. The service doesn't have to be aggressively Victorian. A simple Colonial teapot is authentically Victorian because the Colonial Revival style began in the 19th century.

Victorian society inherited a rich gaming tradition from the 18th century, and it thrived amongst the upper classes, as seen in this illustration. It is also a good catalogue of Victorian male facial hair styles.

CASINO NOW MEANS ONE OF THE GLITTERING gambling palaces in Las Vegas or Atlantic City; but Victorians used it in its earlier and more prestigious sense as an elegant country club house or summer house, usually of one story, for various kinds of social events at swank resort areas like Newport, Rhode Island.

Your casino party might concentrate on a celebration of a fashionable Victorian card game like whist—the ancestor of today's contract bridge. In the eighteenth century Edmond Hoyle published his famous "according to Hoyle" rule book about whist, which transformed the popular old English game into a stylish pastime for the upper classes. The most important Victorian guide was the 1862 *Principles of Whist*

by Henry Jones, better known as "Cavendish," a name he took from his favorite London whist club.

Or your casino might explore other Victorian games. In 1890 "Cavendish" also compiled a book about *Patience Games* or what American authors like William B. Dick in his 1884 *Games of Patience* subtitled "Solitaire With Cards." Although patience or solitaire was not designed for social play, there is much to recommend it for a social setting. Many of the games have fascinating names like "The Beleaguered Castle," "The Gathering of the Clans," or "The Sultan of Turkey." The designs of the "disposition of the cards at the commencement of each game" are often handsome. According to Dick, for those who don't like the

head-to-head competition of other card games, there is "no opposing player to thwart your best intentions and ruin your well-planned endeavors with every card you play—you have it all your own way."

To satisfy individual desires at your casino, the widest possible range of card, table, or board games might be made available. In addition to whist or bridge, you might encourage card games like euchre, casino, cribbage, bezique, snap, old maid, poker, or vingt-un. Anagrams was a popular Victorian table game played with special boxes of letters. Boards for checkers or chess might be provided.

If you decide to expand your casino from a private affair for your friends to a public event for fund-raising or consciousness-raising, you might organize a small exhibition of Victorian games, especially board games that are now chic collectibles. One or two of them might be played out at specified times as part of the public display.

Depending on the scheduled time and scale of your casino, the food might range from a simple dessert akin to an old-fashioned ice-cream social, to an elaborate dessert party, to a small supper climaxed by elegant desserts.

The nicest way to check a game of chess is to break for dessert (left). Victorians made standard board games and decks of cards in all levels of quality from the most vulgar to the most exquisite. All are collectible today, along with more ephemeral board and card games of the period (right).

AN AFTERWORD

It has been greatly rewarding to tease from the yellowed cards and notebook pages and faded handwriting the secrets of grandmother's blackberry cake or Aunt Irma's sour cream twists or mother's peach coffee cake and to savor again the extraordinary desserts I so loved as a child.

Jim Fobel's Old-Fashioned Baking Book, 1987

MY PARTY IS OVER AND YOURS IS ABOUT TO begin. I hope I have opened the shutters on the Victorian Epoch and shed some light on some of the darkness it acquired in the twentieth century.

In a decade, more or less depending when you read this, "our" twentieth century will be over and belong, like that of the Victorians, to history. It is imperative that you try to preserve what you can of your family's Victorian heritage. We are the last generation of the twentieth century to have any contact with the Victorians through the memories of our parents and grandparents. When they are gone, the link will be broken.

The best way to keep that link alive is with food. Try to find out what your Victorian family ate. When one of your family's estates is broken up, let others squabble over the furniture, pictures, and silver. Head for the kitchen and hunt for the beat-up cookbooks, fragile newspaper and magazine recipes, and scrawled recipes stained with evidence of use. There you will find your family heritage. Use it as the basis for questioning the surviving older members of your family; then compile your own cookbook that can be handed down to future generations in the next century.

As much as possible, I have let Victorian words and pictures speak for themselves about Victorian entertaining. In the phrase of a common Victorian entertainment, I hope they have made the Victorians appear more "At Home" and that you now feel more "At Home" with them.

BIBLIOGRAPHY

Adams, Samuel Hopkins. *Grandfather Stories* (New York: Random House, 1955). Delightful tales about growing up in the 1880s in Upstate New York by a master storyteller. "A Third Ward New Year's" is a classic whose drama is centered on the food of Victorian entertainment.

Bailey, Adrian. *Mrs. Bridges' Upstairs, Downstairs Cookery Book* (New York: Simon and Schuster, 1974). Written as an imitation of a 1905 book by an expert in the history of British cookery.

Beard, James. *American Cookery* (Boston: Little, Brown & Co., Inc., 1972). One of many American "heritage" cookbooks, rich with the author's memories of growing up in the early twentieth century with Victorian cookery. It is probably the best of its kind.

Beck, Leonard N. *Two "Loaf-Givers" or A Tour Through the Gastronomic Libraries of Katherine Golden Bitting and Elizabeth Robins Punnell* (Washington: Library of Congress, 1984). Thoroughly researched and wonderfully written history of gastronomic literature.

Beecher, Catharine E. and Harriet Beecher Stowe. *The American Woman's Home* (New York: Ford, 1869). In a new introduction by Joseph Van Why, Executive Director of the Stowe-Day Foundation, this book is called "the Sears-Roebuck catalogue of domestic and moral standards of a century ago." Mostly written by Catharine Beecher, it appeared in various editions. To better position this moralistic tract in the more familiar Victorian domestic "cope" books, the edition for 1873 was titled *The Housekeeper's Manual* and was enlarged at the back with Catharine Beecher's *Handy Cook Book*. The Stowe-Day Foundation has a paperback version of the first edition.

Beeton, Isabella. *The Book of Household Management* (London: S.O. Beeton, 1861). This is the most famous single-volume Victorian "cope" book, which provided the model for countless successors. It has never gone out of print, although it has been revised a number of times. The best remains the first edition, which is currently available in an expensive paperback form.

Belden, Louis Conway. *The Festive Tradition: Table Decorations and Desserts in America, 1960–1900* (New York: Norton, 1983). Solid, beautiful, and entertaining—a paragon of food history books, the best of its kind.

Berkowitz, Bill. *Local Heroes* (Lexington, Massachusetts: D.C. Heath, 1987). A guide to "building community life" with case studies that might serve as models for using Victorian entertainment to achieve the same goal.

Black, Naomi. *Seashore Entertaining* (Philadelphia: Running Press, 1987).

Coleman, Anne Beckley (comp.). *Winterthur's Culinary Collection* (Winterthur Museum, 1983). Mostly contemporary recipes submitted by the Winterthur Museum guides and staff. There are sections on historic background as well as some historic recipes from the museum library, but the best part is the "Reminiscence" by Henry Francis duPont's daughters. It reminds us that this family, which was one of the wealthiest in America and could have anything to eat, lived on "a working farm" and "ate heart, liver, sweetbreads, and tongue as a matter of course. Mother was especially fond of tripe and Father of pig's feet, and to this day we still like them." In other words, they ate in the Victorian manner.

David, Elizabeth. *English Bread and Yeast Cookery* (New York: Viking, 1980). Quite simply the best bread book in English, wonderfully researched and written—a tour de force.

_____. *An Omelette and a Glass of Wine* (New York: Viking, 1985). A compilation from 35 years of magazine writing about food and cookery by one of the world's best practitioners, who is credited with transforming postwar Britain's cookery from the depths to the heights.

Dickens, Charles, *A Christmas Tree*. This can be found in any edition of his collected works.

Drury, Elizabeth. *The Butler's Pantry Book: A Compendium of Household Secrets from the Victorian Age* (New York: St. Martin's, 1981).

Fisher, M.F.K. (trans.). *Brillat-Savarin's Physiology of Taste* (New York: Knopf, 1971). First published as a limited edition in 1949, this is the most famous gastronomic guide of the nineteenth century translated by one of the best gastronomic authors of the twentieth century. The French Revolution made Brillat-Savarin too hot for his own good, so he hid out in America until he cooled down, and it was safe to return to France. His experiences are reflected in this book, published a few weeks before his death in 1826.

Fitzgibbon, Theodora. *A Taste of Scotland: Scottish Traditional Food* (London: Dent, 1970).

Fobel, Jim. *Jim Fobel's Old Fashioned Baking Book: Recipes from an American Childhood* (New York: Ballentine Books, 1987). Excellent example of a personal family heritage cookbook assembled by a professional. It can be used as a model for others wanting to preserve the Victorian and Edwardian food histories of their families and put them into a form that can be handed down to succeeding generations.

Freeman, Sarah. *Isabella and Sam: The Story of Mrs. Beeton* (New York: Coward, McCann and Geoghegan, 1978). Well-researched and written biography of Isabella Beeton. With extraordinary energy and despite the duties of attending to brothers, sisters, her own children, and a husband who used her mercilessly to build his publishing house, she created the Victorian epoch's most widely read domestic "cope" book.

Frey, Iris Ihde. *Crumpet and Scones* (New York: St. Martin's, 1982).

Gaskell, G.A. *Gaskell's Compendium of Forms* (Chicago: Fairbanks, Palmer, 1880). Although it was an unsuccessful competitor of *Hill's Manual,* it has some good color plates, wonderful Late Victorian graphics, and much useful information.

Gernsheim, Alison. *Victorian and Edwardian Fashion: A Photographic Survey* (New York: Dover, 1981). More than just a picture book, it is a solidly researched history based on a great private collection of photographs.

The Hammond-Harwood House Cook Book (Annapolis: Hammond-Harwood House Association, 1963). One of the best regional cookbooks that belongs on the shelf of any American cookbook library.

Harwell, Richard Barksdale. *The Mint Julep* (Charlottesville: University of Virginia, 1975).

Henderson, Mary F. *Practical Cooking and Dinner Giving* (New York: Harper, 1876). Excellent compact guide to Victorian entertaining. Mrs. Henderson had studied in England and was a student of Pierre Blot's New York Cookery School; thus she combined professional European training with the American Victorian experience in her St. Louis home.

Hess, John L. and Karen. *The Taste of America* (New York: Grossman, 1977). Excellent, well-researched, iconoclastic history with a section on Eliza Leslie. The bibliography lists the nineteenth-century classics by Acton, Beeton, Blot, Child, Leslie, Lincoln, Parloa, Randolph, and Tyres and notes which of these are available in reprint.

Hill, Thomas E. *Hill's Manual of Social and Business Forms* (Chicago, 1873). By 1890, 340,000 copies of this book were in print. It was the best and most popular book of its kind. Originals used to be cheap but are now expensive. Copies of recent reprints can still be found.

Household Conveniences (New York: Orange Judd, 1884). Rich source of practical advice compiled from *American Agriculturalist.*

Hughes, M.V. *A Victorian Family, 1870–1900* (New York: Oxford University Press, 1946). A trilogy of memories of a girl growing up in Late Victorian London.

Irving, Washington. *Old Christmas.* There were many editions of this section from Irving's *Sketch Book,* first published in 1819. Sleepy Hollow Restorations, which looks after Irving's home at Sunnyside in Tarrytown on the Hudson River, reprinted in 1977 the 1875 Macmillan edition with illustrations by Caldecott. The most handsome edition is the 1908 Dodd, Mead edition with illustrations by Cecil Aldin.

Ivry, Benjamin. *Regatta: A Celebration of Oarsmanship* (New York: Simon and Schuster, 1988).

Lawton, Mary (comp.). *The Queen of Cooks—and Some Kings (The Story of Rosa Lewis)* (Boni and Liverwright, 1925). The memoirs of the real-life "Dutchess of Duke Street" filled with sensible, practical advice from London's most successful Edwardian caterer.

Leslie, Eliza. *New Receipts for Cooking* (Philadelphia: Peterson, 1854). Leslie was the best Victorian cookery author in America; she was the equal of her contemporary in England, Eliza Acton. This book features a large section on Indian meal preparations. There are also bills of fare for various meals, seasons, and kinds of company. Most interesting is the following credit given in her introduction to Negro cooks: "Many were dictated by colored cooks, of high reputation in the art, for which nature seems to have gifted that race with a peculiar capability."

Leopold, Allison Kyle. *Victorian Splendor: Re-Creating America's 19th-Century Interiors* (New York: Stewart, Tabori, and Chang, 1986). A beautiful book, extensively researched and beautifully written.

Malone, Dorothy. *How Momma Could Cook!* (New York: Wyn, 1946). This is a delightful tribute to the delicious food made by her Late Victorian mother, perhaps the first example of a published "Victorian family heritage" cookbook. Perhaps the introduction is the source of the often repeated remark that "Momma's parties always ended up in the kitchen, as all successful parties always do."

Nearing, Helen and Scott. *The Maple Sugar Book* (New York: John Day, 1950). Maple sugar is indisputedly a North American product and Victorians used it extensively. Today, the mystique of maple sugar has risen with its price; this is an early, thorough, and fervent guide to its use in cookery.

Neil, Marion Harris. *A Calendar of Dinners with 615 Recipes* (Cincinnati: Proctor & Gamble, 1913). Seasonal cookbooks and calendars of meals appeared before the nineteenth century, but the Victorians relied on them more extensively than their predecessors did. *Beeton's Book of Household Management,* for example, has such a list at the back. Books like this one promoting Crisco cooking oil, were part of an attempt by corporate food processors like Proctor & Gamble to take control of home cooking.

Original Menus (Rochester, New York: Curtice Brothers, 1910). An exceptionally handsome and colorful example of a tinned food producer's recipe book. It strains the limits of credulity, however, by attributing "originality" to recipes that are largely poured out of bottles, jars, and cans! The company is still in existence as Curtice-Burns, primarily a private-label canner.

O'Neil, Sunny. *The Gift of Christmas Past: A Return to Victorian Traditions* (Nashville: American Association for State and Local History, 1981).

Parloa, Maria. *Miss Parloa's New Cook Book and Marketing Guide* (Boston: Estes and Lauriat, 1880). She was Principal of The School of Cooking in Boston.

Practical Housekeeping (Minneapolis: Buckeye Publishing, 1881). Better known as *Buckeye Cookery* and first published in 1878, by 1880 100,000 copies of this classic had been sold. The publisher noted in the 1881 edition that "all its local features [have been] dropped, and with them now disappears that part of the title which identified the book with the state where it originated"—a sad commentary on the destruction of regional traditions in the late-nineteenth century.

Ranhofer, Charles. *The Epicurean* (New York: Ranhofer, 1893). Ranhofer was the chef of Delmonico's in New York. In addition to a professional encyclopedia of food preparation, there are 512 bills of fare for various months, numbers of guests, and meals as well as a selection of bills of fare from the period 1862 to 1893. Recently, Dover did a paperback reprint.

Ray, Elizabeth (comp. and ed.). *The Best of Eliza Acton* (London: Longmans Green, 1968). Available in a Penguin edition since 1974. Selections from Acton's 1845 *Modern Cookery for Private Families,* with an introduction by Elizabeth David.

Root, Waverly. *Food* (New York: Simon and Schuster, 1980). A one-volume, wonderfully written encyclopedic reference book.

Rorer, Mrs. S.T. *Philadelphia Cook Book: A Manual of Home Economies* (Philadelphia: Arnold, 1886). Read the subtitle carefully. This is not an early example of a Late Victorian "Home Economics" cookbook in the tradition of Fanny Farmer; it's a late example of the Early Victorian "Home Economies" cookbook. Mrs. Rorer was the Principal of the Philadelphia Cooking School, and Mrs. Rorer's school taught cooks instead of "home economists."

Roth, Rodris, "Tea Drinking in America: Its Etiquette and Equipage," *U.S. National Museum Bulletin 225* (Paper 14, pages 61–91, 1916). This Smithsonian Institution publication is the best on the subject, characteristic of the author's high standards of scholarship and writing.

Rybczynski, Witold. *Home: A Short History of an Idea* (New York: Viking, 1986). Ground-breaking history of the middle-class idea of home with important emphasis on the Dutch contribution, which formed the background of Victorian entertaining.

Schlesinger, Arthur M. *Learning How to Behave: A Historical Study of American Etiquette Books* (New York: Macmillan, 1946). This classic study by a great American historian, not to be confused with his junior, is a safe distance from the witchery of old etiquette books.

Sloat, Caroline (ed.). *Old Sturbridge Village Cookbook: Authentic Early American Recipes for the Modern Kitchen* (Chester, Connecticut: Globe Pequot, 1984). Carefully researched revival of selected recipes and advice from Lydia Maria Child's popular *American Frugal Housewife,* first published in Boston in 1829.

Sokolov, Raymond. *Fading Feast: A Compendium of Disappearing American Regional Foods* (New York: Farrar, Straus & Giroux, 1981). A selection of pieces by this "writer whose special interests are the history and preparation of food."

Standard American Cookbook (Springfield, Ohio: Crowell & Kirkpatrick, 1986). A compilation of various authors.

Stanton, Florence K. (ed.). *The Practical Housekeeper* (Philadelphia: Keeler & Kirkpatrick, 1989). This compendium is a Late Victorian example of the single-volume Victorian "cope" book sold to inexperienced housewives with large families and no servant help.

Stricker, William F. *Keeping Christmas: An Edwardian Age Memoir* (Owings Mills, Maryland: Stemmer, 1981). Christmas in Baltimore, lovingly, but accurately described by a prominent prelate who was H.L. Mencken's neighbor.

Tyree, Marion Cabell. *Housekeeping in Old Virginia* (Louisville, Kentucky: Favorite Recipes Press, 1965). Reprint of the 1879 classic.

Wheaton, Barbara Ketcham (ed.). *Victorian Ices & Ice Cream* (New York: Metropolitan Museum, 1976). Selections from A.B. Marshall's *The Book of Ices* (London, 1885).

Whitehead, Jessup. *The Steward's Handbook and Guide to Party Catering* (Chicago: Jessup Whitehead, 1887). A professional's guide to Victorian entertaining with emphasis on the elaborate forms peculiar to the Late Victorians. In addition to its practical advice and other "tricks of the trade," sharpened by the professional obligation to make money through efficiency, it reveals many details of entertaining that at the time were either left to professionals and servants or were too self-evident to be discussed in "housewifery" books.

Williams, Susan. *Savory Suppers and Fashionable Feasts: Dining in Victorian America* (New York: Pantheon, 1985). Richly documented from the collections of the Strong Museum in Rochester, New York.

Winkler, Gail Caskey and Roger W. Moss. *Victorian Interior Decoration: American Interiors, 1830–1900* (New York: Holt, 1986). Richly documented chronological survey.

Ziemann, Hugo and Mrs. F.L. Gillette. *The White House Cook Book* (Old Greenwich: Devin-Adair, 1983). A reprint of the 1903 edition, first published in 1887. Ziemann was steward of the White House. At the back is a list of menus for a week in each month, holidays, and other special occasions like Mrs. Cleveland's Wedding Lunch (June 4, 1888) and General Grant's Birthday Dinner.

SOURCES

The world of Victorian entertaining is so vast that only a few regions of further exploration can be suggested here. Begin by asking questions of other Victoriana lovers. Or find them in the more than 4,000 preservation societies in North America. For information about those near you contact **The National Trust for Historic Preservation,** 1785 Massachusetts Avenue, NW, Washington, DC 20036 or Heritage Canada, P.O. Box 1358 Station B, Ottawa, Ontario K1P 5R4. **The Victorian Society in America,** based at 219 South Sixth Street, Philadelphia, PA 19106, has regional chapters. As a contributing editor to **Victorian Homes** magazine, I'm prejudiced, but it's the best source of information about real Victoriana for real people (P.O. Box 61, Miller's Falls, MA 01349).

Ecclesiastes would say today, "Of the making of catalogues, there is no end." The three best museum catalogues with significant Victoriana are **The Smithsonian Institution,** Washington, DC 20013, **The Metropolitan Museum of Art,** Middle Village, NY 11381, and **Museum of Fine Arts,** P.O. Box 1044, Boston, MA 02120.

The best cook's catalogue is **Williams-Sonoma**, P.O. Box 7456, San Francisco, CA 94120. The best catalogue for gardeners is **Smith & Hawken,** 25 Corte Madera, Mill Valley, CA 94941. A personal favorite for decorative items is **The Paragon,** Tom Harvey Road, Westerly, RI 02891. **The Vermont Country Store,** P.O. Box 3000, Manchester Center, VT 05255 has practical items.

The best direct merchant of furnishings and fashions for romantic living is Laura Ashley. Unlike other mass-merchandisers, Laura Ashley's products are an integrated system that links paints, wallpapers, textiles, and ceramics with color as well as design. (**Laura Ashley by Post,** P.O. Box 891, Mahwah, NJ 07430-9990)

Along with death and taxes, another certainty is that within six months of ordering from a mailorder catalogue you will receive everyone else's. Pay attention to **Wolferman's,** P.O. Box 15913, Lenexa, KS 66215, which features big and exotic muffins with all the trimmings for a romantic tea. **Norm Thompson,** P.O. Box 3999, Portland, OR 97208 features holiday foods like "Mrs. Beeton's Christmas Plum Pudding," shortbread from Scotland, Kentucky Derby Ham, gourmet sausages, and famous Rogers's Chocolate Creams from Victoria, British Columbia. **Omaha Steaks,** P.O. Box 3300, Omaha, NE 68103 can provide a frozen crown roast of pork and other special meat and seafood entrees. If you require a roast suckling pig, you can get one from **Campbell Farms,** P.O. Box 74, Post Mills, VT 05058.

Other useful food products are: Johhnycake Cornmeal from **Kenyon's Cornmeal,** Usequepaugh, RI 02892; Maple Syrup Products from **Maple Grove,** 167 Portland Street, Johnsbury, VT 05819 or **Le Gourmet Canadien,** 988 Elgin Avenue, Winnipeg, Ontario R3E 1B4; Plum Pudding from **Proper Puddings,** 912 President Street, Brooklyn, NY 11215; Hams from **Smithfield Hams,** P.O. Box 487, Smithfield, VA 23430 or **McArthur's Smokehouse,** Main Street, Millerton, NY 12546; **Victorian Victuals,** a line of baked goods designed by Barbara Bushell of Oregon City, OR available at gourmet and gift shops—call 503-650-0840 for a list.

Our century has become addicted to a narrow range of fizzy drinks, but the Victorian tradition of tea and coffee in great variety is alive and well at the following retailers and mail order companies. NEW YORK CITY: **Bell-Bates,** 107 West Broadway, 10013; **Paprika Weiss,** 1546 Second Avenue, 10028; **M. Rohrs,** 1691 Second Avenue, 10028; **Schapira Coffee Company,** 117 West Tenth Street, 10011; **Zabar's,** Broadway at Eightieth Street, 10024. NEW YORK STATE: **Gertrude H. Ford Tea,** P.O. Box 3407, Poughkeepsie 12603; **Schapira's Coffee and Tea,** P.O. Box 75, Ancramdale 12503; VIRGINIA: **First Colony Coffee & Tea,** P.O. Box 11005, Norfolk 23517. CALIFORNIA: **Star Bucks Coffee & Tea,** P.O. Box 8604, Emeryville, 94662; **Graffeo Coffee House,** 733 Columbus Avenue, San Francisco 94133; **East India Tea & Coffee,** 1481 Third Street, San Francisco 94102. CANADA: **Coffees of the World,** 1230 Yonge Street, Toronto, Ontario; **Murchie's Tea & Coffee,** 1008 Robson Street, Vancouver, British Columbia; **Top Banana Indian Tea,** 1526 Merivale Road, Ottawa, Ontario; **Mihamaya Japanese Tea,** 392 Powell Street, Vancouver, British Columbia.

In the last 20 years, reproduction products for furnishing a Victorian home have proliferated. **The Preservation Press** at 1785 Massachusetts Avenue, NW, Washington, DC 20036 has published guidebooks on what is available in fabrics, wallpapers, carpets, and lighting. My favorite specialists are **Bradbury & Bradbury Wallpapers,** P.O. Box 155, Benicia, CA 94510 and **J.R. Burrows & Co.,** Victorian Design Merchants, P.O. Box 418, Cathedral Station, Boston, MA 02118. For wall stencils contact **St. Catherine's Stencils,** P.O. Box 9329, Cincinnati, OH 45209.

Two of the most prominent mail-order suppliers of reproduction Victorian furniture are **Magnolia Hall,** 726 Andover, Atlanta, GA 30327 and **Martha M. House,** 1022 S. Decatur Street, Montgomery, AL 36104.

Four antique dealers specializing in Victoriana known personally to me are: **Joan Bogart,** 1392 Old Northern Boulevard, Roslyn, NY 11576; **Richard & Eileen Dubrow,** P.O. Box 128, Bayside, NY 11361; **Mimi Findlay,** 1556 Third Avenue, New York, NY 10028; **Steptoe & Wife,** 322 Geary Avenue, Toronto, Ontario M6H 2C7. For antique wicker, contact **Mary Jean McLaughlin,** c/o A Summer Place, 29 Whitfield Street, Guilford, CT 06437. Most major newspapers run a special auction section each week; many auction houses put serious buyers on their mailing list. Antique shows and flea markets are also good places to find specialists.

Lace is synonymous with Victorian. There are many suppliers: **Rue de France,** 78 Thames Street, Newport, RI 02840; **Wecker Textiles,** P.O. Box 212, Punta Gorda, FL 33950; **London Lace,** 167 Newbury Street, Boston, MA 02116; **European Lace,** 24 Mills Plain Road, Danbury, CT 06810; Marquis Lace, 2509 East Thousand Oaks Boulevard, Suite 345, Thousand Oaks, CA 91359; **Victorian House,** 128 Longwood Street, Rockford, IL 61107. A new publication is **Lace Crafts Quarterly,** 3201 East Lakeshore Drive, Tallahassee, FL 32312.

Linens for the table can be had from: **Linen Lady,** 855 Fifty-Seventh Street, Sacramento, CA 95819; **Classic White,** P.O. Box 111, Delafield, WI 53018; The Perfect Setting, 122 Hoodridge Drive, Pittsburgh, PA 15228; **Quaker Lace,** 24 W. Fortieth Street, New York, NY 10036.

The rise in the price of Victorian and freshly minted ornate silver flatware has reduced the general expectation of its use at anything but the most pretentiously formal dinners. Stainless steel patterns that capture the heft of sterling are acceptable substitutes, don't require polishing, withstand mechanical dishwashing, and don't get stolen. Instead of sterling, think of buying a set of nineteenthcentury porcelain from an antique dealer specializing in estate settlements. Fill out the set through matching services like **Replacements,** 302 Gallimore Dairy Road, Greensboro, NC 27409. A specialist is **Haviland Matching Service,** 3959 N. Harcourt Place, Milwaukee, WI 53211.

Discount sources for new china, silver, and crystal are **Ross-Simons,** 136 Route 5, Warwick, RI 02886; **Barrons,** 22790 Heslip Drive, Novi, MI 48050; **Eastside Gifts,** 351 Grand Street, New York, NY 10002; **Thurber's,** 2158 Plainfield Pike, Cranston, RI 02921; **Lanac Sales,** 73 Canal Street, New York, NY 10002.

Dressing your table for a Victorian entertainment is easier than dressing yourself. The best sources for patterns and accessories are **Amazon Dry Goods,** 2218 East Eleventh Street, Davenport, IA 52803 and **Past Patterns,** P.O. Box 7587, Grand Rapids, MI 49510.

Sources for colorful Victorian stickers, cards, and other paper products are **Victorian Ventures,** P.O. Box 341, Montclair, NJ 07042; **Paper Potpourri,** P.O. Box 5575, Portland, OR 97228; **Federal Smallwares,** 85 Fifth Avenue, New York, NY 10003. For your own Victorian calling cards, contact **M'Lady's Printer,** P.O. Box 141112, Cleveland, OH 44114.

Victorian Christmas parties require special effects. The best source for decorative items is **Sunny O'Neil,** 7106 River Road, Bethesda, MD 20817. A manufacturer of Victorian Christmas tree ornaments is **Wm. J. Rigby,** 3672 Richmond Road, Staten Island, NY 10306. For an extraordinary Christmas party you might hire **Constance Hershey** for her all day, onsite consultation called "Decorating for Christmas," which can include a lecture. She is an expert on the various Victorian styles of decorating trees, tables, and interiors as well as menus and observation of the holiday. She is also an excellent consultant on creating a Victorian Gala. Contact her at 3100 Germantown Pike, Fairview Village, PA 19403.

Victorian entertainments can't have great conclusions in the dining room without great beginnings in the kitchen. That's why serious cooks are addicted to cookery books. The biggest mail-order catalogue of new books is **Jessica's Biscuit,** P.O. Box 301, Newton, MA 02160. The best booksellers are **Kitchen Arts & Letters,** 1435 Lexington Avenue, New York, NY 10128 and **H.T. Hicks,** P.O. Box 462, Haddenfield, NJ 08033.

INDEX

Artwork and Illustrations

Many thanks to the following contributors for the original Victorian art and illustrations shown on the pages listed below.

Courtesy B. Shackman & Co.

5, 6, 7, 12, 14, 17, 25(l), 27, 37, 45(b), 46, 48(l), 54, 74, 98, 106, 108, 119, 127, 128

Courtesy American Life Foundation

8, 12, 20, 21, 23, 25(r), 28, 29, 35, 44, 45(r), 46, 48(r), 51, 52, 55, 57, 60, 70, 74, 81, 82, 85, 86, 93, 94, 100, 105, 106, 109, 111, 114, 116, 123, 130, 131, 137

Silhouetted Photographs

© L. Bartone/FPG International: 93
Courtesy The Bombay Company: 19, 135
© R. Chandler/FPG International: 28
Courtesy Dover Publications, Inc./Artwork by Ralph Caldecott: 16, 126, 133
© Steve Gottlieb/FPG International: 86
© Elizabeth Hibbs/FPG International: 132
© Bill Margerin/FPG International: 41(r), 119
© Steven Mark Needham/Envision: 72, 73, 79, 120
Courtesy The New York Historical Society/Bella C. Landauer Collection: 76
North Wind Picture Archives: 77
© Judd Pilossof: 125
© Ralph B. Pleasant/FPG International: 72
© Guy Powers/Envision: 41
© Martin Rogers/FPG International: 89